The HELP Book

by Raja

(1st edition Published in 1995)

Published by
HELP Books International
P.O. Box 929
Wimbledon - SW19 2AX
London - U.K.
e-mail: helpbooksint@easynet.co.uk
www.helpbooksInt.com

ISBN 0 9535120 0 2

Typeset & Edited by
Vaughan Hawthorne-Nelson & Brian Hill

The HELP Book is based on talks by Raja
Illustrations and cover image conceived by Raja

Printed and bound in England by
Cox & Wyman Ltd., Reading, Berkshire

This book
is dedicated to all of us,
who by helping each other
can make our planet
paradise
here and now.

Contents

The Pathway of Being

The Pathway of Knowing

The Pathway of Relating

HELP!

Help! This very word is one of the most commonly used in human existence, even more common than money, time, love and God. How many times a day do you see, hear or use the word help in some way? All organisations, institutions, religions and social services depend on their *help* lines to serve their customers. Today the word *help* will appear in many languages on millions of TV's, radios, computers and signposts across the world.

Why is help so universal?

Everyone needs help each day, whether it be in a crisis or simply as a *helping hand* to make life easier. To most people *help* suggests giving assistance to a stranger, family or friend, but is there more to help than this? How many of us have ever thought about how often we use the *interaction* of help, not only in passing, but to stay alive? For example, breathing, eating and bathing are all interactions of help, between ourselves and the Earth. H.E.L.P.* is a life-force that sustains all life forms. Once you have become aware of HELP, you will notice how often the word *help*, and the interaction of help, is used in daily life.

If help is the way to stay alive, then our every idea, thought and action is an attempt to help ourselves, other living things and the Earth. But, if everything we do is an attempt at helping, then why is our species in crisis, with billions of people suffering? Yes, that is true, but we can use help to improve *every* situation and human condition you can think of. If so, then help is the key activity that will overcome every adversity within humanity. Can you think of a more *practical solution* than that?

*H.E.L.P. stands for Human Evolution & Life Procreation and will be referred to throughout the text as HELP to separate it from the everyday use of the word 'help'.

The human crisis is a massive problem, but the solution is simple. HELP! Our world is in such a poor condition because we do not know how to help either ourselves, other living things or the Earth. This may sound too simple. It *is* simple. HELP is the answer to our crisis and the more each one of us understands how to give and receive help, the more peace, ease and progress there will be in every aspect of human existence. Imagine what you could create if you had all the help you needed.

The reason we cannot give and receive *all* the help we need, is that we understand very little about it. Countless self-help books have been written, but what do you know about the greater potential of help and how it works? The more you *understand* how help works, the more you can *use* it to help yourself fulfil every need, want and wish. Whereas a self-help book treats a particular problem, the HELP book will help you to give and receive help exactly at your point of need.

HELP is the ultimate "self-help" book!

Think about it. What if the interaction of HELP was governed by a process that can be learnt, taught and practised with absolute mastery? This is exactly what has been discovered and is explained in this book. Each chapter will develop a different aspect of your practice of HELP, so that you can build a complete picture of The HELP Process as you go through the book. Once you have learnt to use The HELP Process, you can help yourself in every situation.

As you read this book you will discover the supernatural potential of HELP and its role of helping humanity and the Earth. The idea of discovering HELP may appear too obvious when compared to other discoveries such as X rays, the speed of light and human DNA, but *think again*. You may ask, "*isn't help common sense?*" Yes, but not The HELP Process. If you look at evolution, things often change in big leaps. Somebody finds a new way or a new innovation and suddenly we wonder, "*why haven't we seen that before?*" The obvious is the most difficult to discover. For example, we have experienced the effects of gravity for thousands of years, but it was the *discovery* of the Laws of Gravity that enabled us to put humans on the moon and in outer space. Let us apply the same thinking to the discovery of The HELP Process. We have all experienced help but we have yet to understand the process. If you had discovered a new way that would help our species in science, art, education, religion and evolution, what else would you call it? The HELP Process will help humanity in every aspect of our existence. Does that make HELP the ultimate discovery? Where other discoveries are often surpassed as we evolve, help is help and will always be ...help.

Because we use the word *help* everyday, we think we know what it means and cannot understand how someone can discover HELP. According to the dictionary help means, 'assistance'. Now compare help as you know it with Human Evolution & Life Procreation. The discovery of HELP is not just a new meaning of the word, but the actual *purpose, process* and *practice* of HELP in the bigger picture.

HELP is an unusual discovery and it will take a while for us to fully understand and use its limitless potential. Looking at our past, we can see that when people help each other, the impossible becomes possible, and yet so often we turn to help as a last resort. How often do *you* ask or offer help? Imagine what would happen to us as individuals, communities and nations if we turned to HELP as the *first* resort.

Many people want to help create a better world, but feel alone, unable and helpless. The HELP book shows us how, by using a simple process that is helping individuals around the world to survive, solve problems, prosper and evolve. In the future, HELP will become a natural part of human existence. Why? Because HELP is a key activity that enables us to create everything we can imagine. Our aim is to make HELP available worldwide.

HELP

in the

Big Picture

Overview

Over three billion years ago life first appeared in the seas of the infant Earth. Four hundred million years ago, living creatures left the protective waters to begin life on land. About two million years ago the earliest humans began to walk upright.

Over the past hundred thousand years intelligence developed and, as a result, in the past forty thousand years came the word, the wheel, the laws of gravity, electricity, and the space craft. From fishlike creatures, to knuckle walkers and then to space travellers, every step, leap and discovery in our evolutionary journey has been made possible by *helping each other*.

Help promotes Human Evolution & Life Procreation.

Humans are one of the most fragile creatures on Earth, and yet we have come to dominate the whole planet. We have done this by inventing tools and by helping each other to survive, solve problems and procreate. Helping each other has been the secret, but *what is the origin of help*? Before humans began to live in groups they must have had the idea of helping each other, from which we have the *yell* or *call* for help! Could help have originated from such a yell, just as a newborn baby cries for help? Was *help* the first word and activity created by the first humans?

Help has been the most primal activity and has been used so commonly that we take it for granted. So far, humans have used help instinctively, but now we have discovered HELP – the driving force of evolution. Over the ages, a yell has become a word, a tool, a concept and a process that governs the whole spectrum of help. This book gives practical guidance on The HELP Process and how each one of us can use it to free ourselves from suffering,

17

struggle and crisis, to evolve more consciously into higher beings.

The wonderful thing about HELP is that it nurtures *everything* in creation. HELP is eternal, manifesting in everything, everywhere in the cosmos. Help not only promotes human evolution, but also the procreation of life in all its forms. Every living thing evolves through the process of HELP and all of creation is connected by the force of HELP, the harbinger of life and love.

HELP has relevance for, and reaches many more species than those on Earth. The 'call' for help crosses *all* frontiers, beyond time and space into other dimensions of existence and returns to us. This is why we pray, '*God* help us*'. The human species has cried out for help and HELP is what has come back.

The discovery of HELP marks the beginning of a new epoch. At this stage of our evolution we shall use HELP to overcome the current crisis and evolve. Future generations will look back from another epoch, another planet, another dimension and see the discovery of HELP as the pivotal point in human evolution.

From the dawn of creation to the present day our species has been using the activity of help to survive, live, procreate and evolve. Helping ourselves is so much a part of living that we take it for granted. Each one of us uses help in infinite ways, but what do we know about how help works?

***What if the activity of help was guided by a process
which governed the whole spectrum of HELP?***

Why, you may ask, do we need to know how help works when our species has been using it from the dawn of creation? For example, we have known for thousands of years that apples fall to the ground. That is common sense, but the discovery of the laws of gravity are not. Today understanding the principles of gravity has led us to space flight and to relate the complexities and the

---

* God, the omnipresent being is at the heart of everything, here, there and everywhere.

nature of space and time. Who knows where the discovery of gravity will lead us in another thousand years?

Before the discovery of The HELP Process, our species had been using it instinctively just like any other forms of life on Earth. Of course we can go on using it like this, but help has unlimited powers, some of which cannot be harnessed by instinctive application alone. To explore the potential of HELP, I would like to ask you these questions:

Do all living things need and use HELP?

Yes. Choose any living thing and you will find that it needs and uses help to survive and reproduce. Furthermore, the more evolved a form of life becomes, the more it uses the medium of HELP to evolve and procreate. A dolphin, for example, needs help and helps other dolphins far more than a jelly fish. So HELP, the most fundamental and primal activity, is in use by all living things.

Is HELP governed by one universal process?

Building upon the notion that all life forms need and use HELP, we can assume that a process of practising HELP does exist. Everything we do is governed by process, e.g. when we build a house we lay the foundations, build the walls and roof, followed by the windows and doors etc. In the same way, HELP is guided by a universal process.

How does the activity of HELP actually work?

When I ask people a simple question, "how does HELP work?" I see either a blank face or a vague reaction such as, "by helping". This is an understandable reaction, since humanity is not aware of what HELP is, let alone how it works. Why do we need to know how HELP actually works? Only by knowing how help works, can we use the medium of HELP with mastery. For instance, if you have only learnt to speak a language but cannot read or write it, your practise of it will be very limited.

The purpose of asking these questions is to promote a new understanding of the use of HELP. The HELP Process is not a belief system that you believe in or belong to. It is a process that you understand and use. The word *understand* means *to know that which you stand upon.* So, as I explain how HELP works, question how the interaction of help will improve your situation *here and now.*

I have met many people who practise methods that promise health, happiness, enlightenment and unlimited wealth, but cannot manifest their intent. Why? Because they do not know the way to get the help they need, to overcome that which is preventing them from manifesting. Are you struggling with negative patterns, addictions, obstacles, lack and limitation? Learning how to give and receive all the help you need will enable you to overcome *all* challenges.

For example, every addiction comes from unfulfilled needs. The process of HELP will fulfil all your needs. Once you have learnt The HELP Process, you will use it to fulfil every need, want and wish. Being able to give and receive help here and now in every interaction and situation will make you an unlimited being.

Becoming an unlimited being will be one of many results of your practise of HELP. As you help yourself and each other, you will feel at peace and ease. The more you give and receive help, the more you will increase peace and ease until you experience paradise. The central aim and purpose of the discovery of HELP is to create **Pan Paradise** on Earth.

The Discovery of HELP

Many people have asked me how I came to discover HELP. Over a lifetime, is the answer. Looking back I can see that since the moment of my birth my whole life has been guided for the sole purpose of discovering HELP. Every discovery has a purpose and the discovery of HELP will help humanity move from hunter-hunted to helper-helped.

I believe that all key discoveries are guided by a cause set in motion from the very beginning of creation. As humanity unfolds, more is discovered to help us move to the next stage of our evolutionary journey. Nothing is discovered by chance. How many generations did it take for example, to prepare for the discovery of gravity? All discoveries are a result of the collective effort of humanity and therefore cannot be credited to one individual.

The Discovery of HELP is a very exact event.

So although 'I' discovered HELP, it was the result of millions of years of preparation as well as the role played by other people and the planet. Humanity is like a river that knows the way to evolve and uses discoveries to weave and wind around obstacles and overcome challenges. With every discovery, we add momentum to the evolutionary journey of humanity. Look back at the past few thousand years and you will see how one discovery led to another as a chain of cause and effect. A good example is the discovery of galaxies beyond our solar system which have recently been photographed by the Hubble telescope. This telescope is the culmination of a chain of events initiated by the pioneer, Galileo.

Evolution appears so random to us because we are not in tune with 'real time' and providence. A discovery is a result of a deliberate chain of events, even to the point of appointing an individual to make that discovery. The easiest way I can explain this is by using the process of conception. When the male ejaculates inside the female vagina, all the sperm come together and help each other to swim to the egg. In the same way, a discovery is the result of this kind of support in the life of an individual.

Here is a classic example. There was once a boy who was rejected from school for being 'backward'. His mother took it upon herself to educate her child as best she could. This very same boy went on to discover the theory of relativity and the speed of light. His name was Albert Einstein. Both his rejection from school and his mother's support were co-operating factors in helping him to reach the point of discovery.

In my own life, I view the help of my mother as well as her early death as co-operating totally in the discovery of HELP. There have been many major and minor events that have led me to this discovery. For me to explain how I discovered HELP, I must tell you about some events from my life.

Being Born.

I was born close to the sea, on the east coast of Tanzania, near a place called Dar-es-Salaam which means, 'a haven for peace'. My birth was at 4:44 am when the sky is at its darkest, just before the dawn. The dawn there is very dramatic since the sun rises to the sound of crashing waves on Oyster Bay. Africa on the whole is a very dramatic continent with its wide open spaces, varied terrain and abundance of life. The environment in East Africa is one of the most natural habitats for human existence. It is believed that the first humans evolved on The Plains of Tanzania.

Being born and raised in such a supportive, natural place has played a crucial role in my life. Nature, more than anything has given me *the power and wisdom to act.* I spent most of my infant days playing in the wilderness where I very rarely wore any clothing. My mother encouraged me to absorb the power of nature by simply allowing me to play freely. Growing up in Dar-es-Salaam was very easy. I can imagine how our ancestors just lived from the land by foraging and sleeping when the day ended. This could well have been how it was for humanity in the beginning: the Garden of Eden, Paradise. One of the key elements of paradise in any philosophy or religion is *peace.* Look closely at any religion and you will find peace at the top of its agenda. For instance, the greeting in Islam is *Assalaam Aleikum,* meaning *May peace and God's mercy be upon you.* The greeting *Shalom* in Hebrew means *peace* and in Hinduism all prayers end with *Om Shanti* meaning *universal peace.*

My memory of growing up in Dar-es-Salaam can be summed up easily. It is that of being at peace and ease. I can remember the feeling of pure *being* from the time I was an infant. My mother would tell me stories from different religions while I was lying in bed. She would place the palm of her hand on my chest before I went to sleep. It brought me so much peace.

> **We have two hands,**
> **one to help ourselves and**
> **the other to help someone else.**

The hands have miraculous powers to transform, heal, build and procreate. I was about seven years of age when I began to identify with peace. Once, while playing in the sand on the beach, my mother came and held my hands. She asked me what I was building. I replied, "Dar-es-Salaam". I will always remember the look on her face as I said that. A few days earlier I had asked her to show me how to write the words Dar-es-Salaam. She had explained that it means *a house of peace.* Intuitively, I have always known that my work is to bring peace and ease.

My vision of peace and ease is founded upon a dream. At the age of nine I began to have a recurring dream of people encircling the Earth by joining hands. This dream was very special to me as I very rarely had other dreams. I would look forward to having the dream again and make it last as long as I could. I remember once falling asleep in the afternoon and having this same dream. It left me speechless for the rest of the day. After this dream I would feel totally at peace. My body would feel completely relaxed and light.

I still have this dream, although not as often as when I was a boy. Even now, when I look at the image I feel deeply touched and rejuvenated. I could look at it forever. In the dream, the people around the Earth glow like golden light beings. They are pure and whole in nature. I call them ***Pan Human*** beings because of their purity of existence and wholeness of being.

For me, the holding of hands round the Earth represents unity and the harmony of humanity helping each other, all living things and the Earth. I see a beautiful bearer of life, a paradise existing in the vastness of space and I live upon it. The whole image signifies creation on every level of existence, created by what I call The Infinite Being who is represented by ⊙ the symbol* which means, 'the one and infinite'.

Every time I have this dream and contemplate on the image, I learn more of what it feels like to live, and imagine a world at ease and living in peace. By sharing this dream with you, I open my heart and mind to let you enter deep within the dream and the origin of the discovery of HELP. My soul purpose of being alive is to help humanity find a living peace.

The dream and image of humans encircling the Earth is symbolic of HELP. My aim is to pass on the idea and action of HELP to all those who wish to know and are willing to help.

*The ⊙ symbol represents 'one and infinity', 'the sun', and is used to denote 'hydrogen' in chemistry.

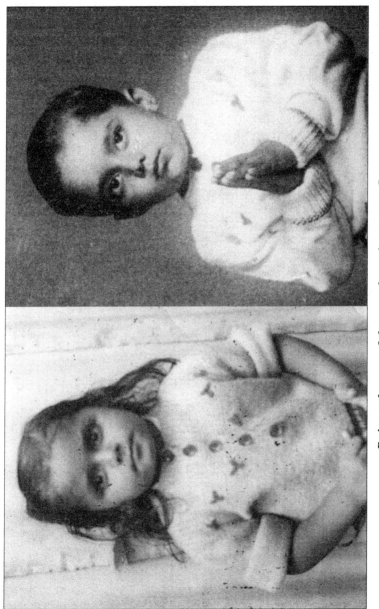

Raja at the age of three and praying at age five.

Raja's mother, Damyanti. She was named after a queen in Indian folklore who showed extraordinary kindness to her people.

Help is the fountain of love and life.

Helping is an ability that can be developed like any other. The secret is willingness. My ability to help was developed when my mother contracted cancer. Soon afterward, she was bedridden and everything had to be done for her. The action of helping my mother during her last years, as she was wasting away, taught me more about life and love than any religion or education.

My mother was an uneducated woman who always helped others. I recall one very hot day, when a black man collapsed on the street in front of the Hindu temple. Whilst everyone held back and watched, she rushed to his aid with some 'holy water' ...to *help* him. This act was very courageous because it was taboo for a Hindu woman from the highest Brahmin cast to touch an untouchable let alone nurse a black stranger. The black people in Africa are considered worse than the untouchables (Harijans) by the Hindus from India. The Hindus would claim to be devoted to the service of God, but would not help a fellow black human being.

This incident made a deep impression on my view of Hinduism and race at a very young age, especially when my mother was shunned by other Brahmins as having tainted herself. In addition, most of my friends were black, and Hindu parents would not allow me to play with their children. I believe that race and religion have become the greatest obstacles to us helping each other. Even those who belong to the same religious order are held back from helping fellow human beings who are suffering because of racial differences. My mother went beyond race and religion, as she would often invite black people to our home and give them food. She was renowned for her kindness and showed me how to help others. Although she was uneducated, she had a purity of being which radiated from her body. Her every action was in some way helpful to others. The accumulation of countless helpful actions had charged her body with love.

> ### *The one legacy my mother left to me,*
> ### *was that of helping others.*

She died when I was fourteen years of age. My mother was the most precious person in my life. When she died I was devastated. The feelings of sadness and pain in my heart were emotionally crippling, as anyone who has lost a loved one knows. During the following months, deep depressions and thoughts of suicide were constantly in my mind. Somewhere inside me, I knew that the way to survive was to master my *will* and walk away on my own.

Day after day, I faced the fears and uncertainties that ran riot in my mind. It was as though my body was paralysed and my mind was a prisoner, and yet I felt that the moments leading to my release were near.

The time came for me to get up, make my way to the door, and step out on to the street. These few steps from my bed on to the street felt like an eternity.

I walked The Sacred Steps.

Now I call them *The Sacred Steps*, because every step was taken with courage, faith and will. Anyone who has become a free person has in some way walked The Sacred Steps. Becoming free from anything is a sacred act of self help. *Only you can set yourself free.* Although I had used a sacred act to set myself free, it would take another decade to understand the role of *self help* in the quest for freedom. For that moment I had used one of the most powerful acts to step on to the street. Little did I know that the same process would serve me time and again on the journey of life-discovery. Being free felt good, but life without a home and family was far from easy. For four years I lived a nomadic existence travelling and working along the way. It was not long before having no roof over my head, lack of affection and poor food took their toll on my body and psyche. Going into the unknown *alone*, day after day drove me into a downward spiral of desperation. The day came when I cried out, *"help me"*, from the core of my being. I was helpless and as I sat alone, a voice from deep within my*self* said, *"help yourself"*. Asking myself for help was the pathway to my Infinite Being. Helping my*self* opened the door to unlimited love, power, wisdom and the grace of God. God *helps those who help themselves.*

In the coming years, it dawned on me that helping myself was the way to a bright and prosperous future. Almost every day I would talk to myself and gain insights into *The Way of HELP.* This led to the discovery of The Foundations of HELP, *Health, Home, Family* and *Work*, whose significance I shall explain later. Looking back, I realise that these foundations became my focus in life, but what I needed was a sense of place where I could build these foundations.

> *I had reached a crossroads in my life where the only choice was either to join the marines, or a monastery.*

I joined the Royal Marines and on passing out, was assigned to the Mountain and Arctic warfare commandos in Scotland. Apart from hostility towards my colour, life was much easier than being on the street: it allowed me to excel in the armed forces. Having a roof over my head and decent food encouraged me to delve deeper into The Way of HELP. The dual existence of being a soldier and a pioneer of a new way was an ideal setting for gaining insights into two completely opposite ways of existence, which I refer to as hunter-hunted and helper-helped.

The Royal Marines became my family and the Condor Commando base in Scotland was my home, enabling me to develop my health and work. In addition to that, the nature of soldiering reunited me with the wilderness where I could develop my understanding of The HELP Process. The armed forces taught me how to take care of myself in *any* situation. I learnt how to do the seemingly impossible, and soon excelled, so that I was assigned to secret organisations. Living and working in a mission critical environment enabled me to develop my devotion and a monastic way of life. These traits make it possible for me to make things happen for the benefit of humanity and the Earth. One major obstacle for many so called 'spiritual people', is their inability to regulate the physical world, i.e., to make things happen in their personal and social settings.

Having been trained as a soldier I wanted to use my art to help people in war torn areas. My aim was not to kill, but to help innocent men, women and children with relief, medical care and evacuation. Although war is destructive, for me it was an opportunity to practise my skills for the service of others. In war, people are really helpless and helping them was my way of relieving their suffering. War made me aware of the connection between help and love. I discovered that the more I helped people, the more they and I became filled with feelings of love.

> *Love is not an idea, song, action or solution.*
> *Love is a feeling created via an act of help.*

Without help, there is no love. When we help ourselves and others, we create feelings of love for everyone. These feelings of love are what we want most out of life. Many people are unhappy with their lot, not because they do not have enough, but because of the lack of love in their hearts. Not knowing the way to create love drives them aimlessly from dawn to dusk, birth to death, pursuing things and thrills, in the hope of finding love. You may have heard the following lyrics that portray the emptiness of our lives: *"I can't get no satisfaction,"* and *"I still haven't found what I'm looking for."* One only looks for something that is lost.

At the end of a long range reconnaissance patrol. In the background is Sgt. Pete Mitchum – S.B.S. who encouraged Raja to excel.

Raja with his friend and mentor, J. D. Wassall M.B.E.M.M.

(Corps Regimental Sergeant Major, Royal Marine Commandos)

Love is what is lost. Let me tell you the secret of finding love. It is so simple that the human mind normally finds it hard to understand. In war, however, or any life-threatening crisis, our mind becomes focused on staying alive and life itself so simplified that we can grasp the things I am saying here.

Although I am not in favour of war, it is a teacher of love. In a war zone, death is but a heartbeat away and one is left with two stark alternatives – *dead or alive.* To stay alive people have to help each other and the more they help, the more love they generate. Help is a way to feel love.

War is a teacher of love.

Death taught me that I have a given number of days and decades to live. I will help as much as I can before I die. In what turned out to be my final mission, something mystical happened which led me to give up my work as a soldier. In this experience, a voice said to me, *"Being, Being itself."* I remembered this voice as I had heard it say, *"help yourself"*, a decade earlier. Listening to this voice was like someone calling my name to awaken me. There was carnage and the chaos of war all around me. It seemed to be on a different plane of existence as I walked out of the situation.

From then on, it was clear that *Being* was the purpose of my life and my way of being in the world, in turn, connected me to The Infinite Being. For the first time there was a continuous conscious awareness of the aim and purpose of life, which has been with me ever since. The discovery of *Being* opened the gates of reality, as everything in and around me was clear and new. My mind became free of the illusions which had fogged my view of the world. I call this ***Paradise***, because Being is a condition that frees us from fear and illusion: the obstacles to experiencing life as paradise. Very few people have actually witnessed moments of paradise and even fewer live in paradise constantly. This is because we are separated from our own being and are guided instead by fear and illusion. In Being, we are guided by intuition, which originates from The Infinite Being, God. To be guided by intuition is central to The Way of HELP, otherwise our thoughts and actions stem from fear and are harmful. Intuition connects us with The Infinite Being and gives us access to what I call *Direct Knowing*. This occurs in the form of dreams, visions and revelations. Through Direct Knowing I received the guidance and insight that became The Way of HELP and *The Pan Pathways*.

How else can a common man discover such universal truths and solutions for our crisis? The discovery of HELP came from direct knowing. The following statements contain the central message of HELP and that is why you need to know their point of origin.

- *HELP is the way to love.*
- *HELP flows from the heart of God.*
- *HELP is the key to salvation and the way to create Paradise on Earth.*
- *HELP will unite all races and nations to create one world with God.*

I can understand that some of you may not believe that a *real* and *practical* discovery can originate from *direct knowing,* so I ask you to suspend your judgement until I explain its potential. As you can see, these statements are not poems, prophecies or prophetic parables open to individual interpretation. These statements are accountable and will be assessed according to their *practical potential to fulfil their claims*.

So, feel free to use *any* means of assessment. Although I ask you to keep an open mind, it does not really matter. HELP will, in time, change the cynical and open closed minds. Who can deny the potential of HELP for the salvation of humanity and the Earth? To understand and practise The Way of HELP, you will have to discover its workings for yourself. It can be very demanding.

The discovery of HELP and The Pan Pathways too has been very demanding. HELP holds mythical and mystical powers and, although I am happy to receive the knowledge, the acceleration in my understanding and my way of life makes me feel very exposed. Pioneering and discovering HELP meant going into the unknown *daily* and even now feels as though I am free-falling in space. I am sharing this with you, because you too may experience such an acceleration and feel isolated. How can a person who discovered HELP feel alone? You see, HELP is a completely new discovery. HELP does not have a lineage or history or hierarchy that I can draw from, relate to or use to explain its potential. With all due respect, even simple questions such as 'how does help work', leaves the wisest bewildered. Direct Knowing has played a key role in the pioneering of HELP and The Pan Pathways. So, to delve deeper, I spent long periods of time alone and in the wilderness.

Most of my life has been devoted to the pioneering and development of HELP. During this time, I have developed many positive traits, but the one that stands supreme is *faith*. From the beginning, very few people have believed in what I was discovering and so I kept quiet about my work. This was the only way to avoid ridicule, rejection and even sabotage on subtle levels. When I shared what I discovered with spiritual people, priests and holy men, they simply dismissed me. Once in my youth, when I was desperate to share what I had found, I went to see a preacher. At the end of our conversation he said, *"You have no right"*. This left me shattered.

My faith in my-self more than anything, or anyone has kept me moving forward.

The journey of discovery has taken me into spaces, both physically and spiritually extreme, that could only be survived by the belief in my*self*. I believe that when people are faithless, they become powerless. Even if people do not believe or understand what I am saying, my faith will continue to stand by me. The discovery of HELP has been powered by faith, which seems to power all acts of creation. The practice of HELP also requires faith, because of the challenges it presents to the practitioner. Many practitioners have told me that they find what I am saying so simple that they do not believe it to be true. When you listen to what I am saying, allow yourself to access the truth by using not only your intellect but also your intuition. *Pray and ask God for guidance.*

I hope that in sharing some of the key events that led to the discovery of HELP, you will be inspired and motivated to begin the practice of HELP. Help is a very powerful and spiritual action that transcends fear and illusion. Help is a selfless act and a person who helps others is a very loving human being. You may be poor, homeless, unemployed, a prostitute, thief or liar, but the moment you help others, your heart will be filled with love. I believe that helping is the ultimate spiritual idea and action, for it brings out *all* the qualities in a human being that are aspired to in the religious texts. Can any quality aspired to by your faith become manifest without helping?

HELP brings forth courage, unity, love, kindness, hope, charity, equality, prosperity, humility, respect, peace, freedom and joy. All these qualities are born of the most simple act of help. Helping is therefore the simplest and most direct route for creating the most ideal condition of existence, the root of all religions and beliefs. Since help is so simple and common, our species has taken it for granted and overlooked its power and potential. HELP has been the silent force behind *every* spiritual doctrine and prophet. Did you know for instance that the name Jesus in Hebrew means, 'He who helps'?

The one who helps is all powerful.

The one who knows how to help changes people's lives for the better, and that leads to love, respect and trust. Help brings out the best in people and when we help each other we ascend to higher levels of existence. It is because people do not know how to help each other that millions of people are suffering. Helping connects us to each other, to living things and to the Earth itself. As long as we remain connected, all our needs and wishes will be fulfilled. The practice of help has brought me from living on the street and eating out of dustbins to having every need met and exceeded before I ask. *God is my helper and provider.*

God has always helped me. Every prayer and every cry for help has always been answered. I am a fortunate man. From the beginning, God has been teaching and training me. The times of trial and tribulation was God showing me what it feels like to be hungry, homeless, without a family and out of work. Without these experiences, how would I know of people's suffering? Ask God to help you. *"God I need you. God help me."* God's help is the source of Divine Strength. HELP is the life-force that flows from the heart of God. Without help from God, we are helpless. Although I discovered HELP, each one of us has to pioneer and practise The Way of HELP in our own way. Look *within yourself* and you will know that what I am saying is true. While you practise The Way of HELP, be patient. Good things often take time. Nature does not rush evolution and your practise of HELP will evolve at its own speed.

It is only a matter of time until HELP is acknowledged and embraced as the key activity in the creation of a bright and beautiful world. This may take several generations, since humans have to evolve from the old way of hunter-hunted, to the new way of helper-helped. Faith and patience will enable our species to evolve naturally into a new kind of being, like the butterfly that naturally changes from one stage to the next.

The discovery and practise of HELP is similar to the development of a butterfly.

From an egg it becomes a caterpillar, then a pupa and finally a butterfly. In my life the dream of people holding hands around the Earth was equivalent to an egg. The next stage was the journey of discovery that represents the nature of the caterpillar. The vision of The Pan Pathways came next where there were unseen developments happening within me. This signifies the motionless period of the pupa. The last stage has just begun as I embark on the diffusion of HELP. This phase, however long it may be, represents the flight of the butterfly*. Just as the butterfly lays it eggs before its death, I want to share The Way of HELP with all those who wish to know of it, before my death.

Out of all the creatures on the Earth, the butterfly is my favourite, because a butterfly is harmless and has no fear. As fragile as it is, the butterfly manages to live and procreate against all odds, often flying for thousands of miles across mountains, deserts and oceans before it lays its eggs. For me the butterfly represents power, beauty, faith and infinite patience. These are qualities that have been paramount in the discovery of HELP. The diffusion of The Way of HELP is also based on the nature of the butterfly, which takes the way of least resistance and conducts its activities in a quiet and peaceful way.

I would like to conclude by sharing my vision of the future. I hope that the discovery of HELP enables our species to live in harmony and create a world living in peace and ease. My dream of the future is that of Paradise on Earth, which can be manifested by each one of us helping ourselves and each other.

---

*Welcome to flight H.E.L.P.!

Who Needs HELP?

There are over five billion human beings on the Earth today. Each one of us is trying to eke out a living on some level or other. By the year 2040 the human population may have doubled to ten billion. Most of us will be alive, but what kind of life will we have? Common sense tells us that the quality of our present living conditions will be halved in all areas. This may be acceptable to some, but for those who are already on the bread line, it spells certain death, unless they can fulfil their basic needs.

Each one of us needs help to make it through daily life, hence the lyric, *"I get by with a little help from my friends."* The kind of help we need however, varies from person to person throughout the world. Wherever we may be living, each one of us needs help in our unique situation. Some need help with medical care, housing and education, others simply need something to eat. Some may need legal advice, therapy for addictions or simply a hug after a hard day. Just as there are infinite needs, there are infinite ways we can give and receive help. The question is: if there are so many ways of helping ourselves and each other, why are so many people still suffering in the world? With so many channels of helping and healing available to us, why isn't humanity at peace and living in a state of paradise?

Millions of people and animals are suffering on the Earth right now, yet we cannot help them. Why?

Is it possible that help is always at hand, but we simply don't know how to get or give it? The world is moving so fast that we have lost the focus on what is really important in our lives. We have lost touch with ourselves and become isolated within the mass of civilisation. We are separate from each other and the Earth because we are separated from our *selves*. We end up living lonely, empty lives and are soon unable to ask for, receive or give help to those who need it. Is it any wonder that the word help is used so often? But what does the word *help* actually mean and what purpose does it serve?

Our first cry for help went out into the world when we were babies in *need,* not only for our mother and her milk, but also her physical affection …touch. Touch, I believe is one of the most basic, primal needs and ways to *feel* love, and that is why holding the hand of someone who is suffering helps *so* much. Our subsequent cries come when we reach points in our lives where we need help to move forward. Most of us at some point in our lives have cried out for help. Even Jesus Christ spoke the following words on the cross:

"God help me"

We tend to think that asking for help is a sign of weakness. If we think of asking for help as a weakness or believe that no one will help us, then our mind will think that we cannot be helped. Instead, our thoughts, emotions and energy will struggle in a vacuum that leads to deep anxiety, worry and stress. These eventually destroy our lives and families. We must understand that everyone needs help sooner or later. No matter how wealthy, independent or powerful a person you may be, without help from others and the Earth, you would be lonely, loveless and suffering. Many are suffering, not as a result of being poor, but because they are deprived of the basic needs of being human. For example, how many of us get *enough* physical affection? Touch is a basic need, just as air, water and food, but we have learnt to go without it, and so desperately yearn to be touched. How many other needs are we deprived of? Over four billion people are living in some form of grief, but how can we possibly help to heal the suffering of so many? The solution to this impossible situation is very simple… *We must ask for help.*

Can you help me?
How can I help you?

The way to relieve all the grief and suffering on the Earth is to *learn* how to help ourselves and each other. Have you ever helped someone in need, or perhaps cried out for help yourself? Did you get it? Helping is not a hit and miss activity, devoid of consciousness. It is a very positive and powerful activity charged with love, compassion, kindness and consciousness. Help is not an activity we only use in times of desperation and crisis. We can use it all the time and anywhere in order to serve others, solve problems and discover new functions, methods and medicines for the benefit of humanity.

Humanity Needs HELP

One look at the condition of humanity reveals how desperate we are and what we are doing to each other, all life forms and the Earth. Clearly, there is a crisis within humanity, hence the widespread suffering. Our struggle to overcome this crisis can only be resolved by people helping each other. So far in the evolution of humanity, relationships have meant competition between individuals and nations, in order to assure their future against scarcity of resources: so we have a world of *haves and have nots*. The new paradigm for the next millennium reiterates that we must make the move from *competition* to *co-operation*. The question is how?

How do we assist each individual in
moving from competition to co-operation?

It is clear that each one of us must learn to co-operate, that is, to help each other, but how can each one of us make that transition?

41

Paradigms can inspire us and platitudes placate us only for a while. The time has come for humanity to take an evolutionary leap from competition (hunter-hunted) to co-operation (helper-helped). What we need is a practical workable process that can be used by *everyone*. The process of HELP fulfils this need and is the stepping stone that will enable humanity to take a quantum leap into the new epoch. Whatever your age, sex, colour, race or religion you can use HELP to unite with others and improve the condition of the Earth.

> ***HELP is one hundred per cent holistic,***
> ***as it unites people in every interaction.***

To help is to unite. Helping each other will be the key activity enabling humanity to unite and create a new world. In every age throughout history, humans have recognised their need and prayed for HELP. Today the need for HELP is perhaps greater than in any other age. It appears that we need help in every aspect of our lives. The need is so desperate that we are listening to any and every source of guidance: looking for UFO's, talking to dolphins, the dead and those with psychic powers. Is there really help *out there*? Well, we have a choice! We can continue to depend on the wise to keep bailing us out, or we can learn to help ourselves. We can wait for the messiah to come and, *'build the Kingdom of Heaven on Earth'*, or we can help each other to create it. Now!

At this critical time we have reached a point where we have become aware of our acute need for help, not just individually but collectively. Our cry implies a crisis that can only be overcome through a spirit of co-operation. This is why the *interaction* of HELP will become the key to co-operation and the prime mover of humanity on individual and collective levels.

What is HELP?

HELP is the discovery of the most *useful* idea, word and action. What is the most common activity *used* by *all* life forms to live and procreate? Choose any need or want and you will have to give and receive help to fulfil it. Even breathing is an interaction of help. Without help we are helpless, and we suffer and die.

The interaction of help begins from the first breath, when God breathes *life* into us. HELP flows directly from the heart of God and that is why help is the *key activity* in all species. God is the source of HELP which will free us from *all* suffering and bondage. What is HELP?

HELP is the key to salvation.

Today humanity is in crisis and we have put the Earth on death row. God wants to help us, but first we must learn to help each other. HELP is the way to save people from crisis. The emergence of HELP is a *providential* discovery that will help humanity in *every* situation of our existence. It will change the way we understand and use help forever. To demonstrate HELP as the key to the salvation of humanity, here are *five* ways of application:

- **HELP is The Way to Survive**

- **HELP is The Way to Live with Love**

- **HELP is The Way to Reunite with God**

- **HELP is The Way to Promote Social Change**

- **HELP is The Way to Promote Human Evolution**

Now I shall explain in more depth the way HELP can be *used* to transform our existence. My aim is to demonstrate that *all* our crises on the personal, communal, national and global levels will be overcome by using HELP.

HELP is The Way to Survive

If you have ever been in a life threatening situation, you will know what it feels like to need help. The cry for help is very powerful, as it comes from the very core of your being. Help has been a primal means by which our species has ensured our survival. We use help not only to survive crises but to stay alive and reproduce.

Help is a primal act of survival.

Over the ages we have survived and thrived because we have learnt how to help ourselves. Everything we learn and experience we use again to help. Take any crisis we have overcome in our past and you will see how help was the solution to our survival. Let me give you an example. During the Black Death plague in 14th Century Europe, thousands of people died daily but many individuals risked their lives to help others survive. Today thousands of individuals risk their lives to help others survive.

An individual has enormous potential to help fellow human beings. HELP harbours primal powers that are usually unleashed in times of crisis. To help in a crisis, we have to transcend our normal behaviour. To do that requires extreme courage and faith, which in turn unleashes the supernatural powers needed to ensure survival. Help is power. The *act of help* is as powerful as the *cry for help*, since it can override one's own need to stay alive.

We help each other to survive in infinite ways, from providing food or giving blood, to calling rescue services and sending money to desperate people. HELP is the way our species has overcome all crises and challenges. It is a natural interaction practised by all forms of life, to survive and procreate. Help is widely practised as a means of survival so that one race will help another, one species will help another and even enemies will help each other, to survive. The simple act of help is the very thread that ties all life forms together.

A few years ago there was an earthquake in Los Angeles, California. Before the disaster, most people of different backgrounds, whites, blacks, gay people, Jews, Muslims, would not mix in their neighbourhoods. The earthquake destroyed buildings, buried people alive, wrecked amenities, fractured roads and created mass panic. When the dust settled, people woke up to the need to help one another, regardless of their colour or creed. By helping each other, their hate turned into love.

As the world becomes smaller and people from different races live side by side, the use of HELP to sustain daily life, becomes more interracial and interactive. Deep down, each one of us knows that we may find ourselves in a crisis, *at any moment.* Help from others is the only way to survive. Let us bring this deep rooted wisdom to the fore and help the distressful condition of humanity and the Earth.

Apart from the threat to our survival created by disease, starvation and wars, we are destroying our natural habitat at a rate four hundred times faster than the damage caused by the biggest meteor that has ever hit the Earth. This is the most dangerous threat to the survival of our species. Should we wait for a crisis to hit us personally before we *wake up* to what is happening?

Many may think this is OK and that cries from across the world can be ignored. This is the greatest folly, for in time, those who ignore a cry for help will in turn be ignored when they are in need. We have to realise that images of children starving on our TV screens are of human beings like you and me. If it were your own child, would you help it to survive? How would you live and what would you sacrifice if they were *your* sons or daughters?

Poverty is one of the biggest threats to our survival. Today, 1.3 billion people live in *dire* poverty, which in turn forces people to use up natural resources, over-populate, breed disease, crime and corruption. I am certain that the key to our survival, both social and environmental, is to show people how they can help each other.

How can we help?

Those of us who are ready and awake, understand that we need to help save our species and the Earth by taking responsibility. For many the question is how? The answer is to do whatever is necessary to help other people, life forms and the Earth, even to the point of risking your own life to help.

HELP is The Way to Live with Love

Every thirty-five seconds, another human being commits suicide. Why? There are many reasons why people take their own life and yet one thing is certain. A person who is suicidal needs HELP. HELP reinstates life and love as it nurtures *every* need of being human. Life and love are inseparable and what we do know is that life is not worth living without love.

The problem is, we don't have enough love. When I was a teenager I used to sing the song, '*All you need is love*'. Love may be all you need, but why was I not overflowing with love? I wanted to generate an abundance of love, but how?

I tried reading books about life and love, but that did not help. I performed rituals and paid homage to holy men, but I still did not learn how to love, so I decided to give up the quest for love. Instead I began to help myself and then others who were in need. In helping people I began to feel love from within me. I realised that the way to love was so simple and easy. By helping people my life overflowed with love, like a fountain. I understood that I had been misled into believing love to be an idea or act. *Love is a feeling.* The feeling of love is created via actions of help. HELP is the mother of all actions of service, kindness and compassion.

Help is an action.
Love is a feeling.

If you look at any story about love, you will see that it is a story about people helping each other. Your own life story will show how you have been loved via actions of help. Think of someone to whom you want to express your love. Even a powerful sentence such as, 'I love you', will need to be followed by helpful actions if your love is to be *felt.* Try refraining from saying the words, 'I love you' to your loved ones for a week; instead help them in every way you can, and then see how they feel towards you.

I have not said 'I love you', to *anyone,* for over two decades. I demonstrate my love by helping others. One of my favourite songs is, 'Nature Boy' sung by Nat King Cole. One of the lyrics is *"The greatest thing you could ever learn is to love and be loved in return."* So true! The question is how do we learn to love? The way to learn to love is by helping people. Every time you perform a helpful action, you help someone feel loved. People feel the extent of your love by the *way* that you help them and vice versa. A parent for instance learns to love by helping their child in every single way. The child in turn learns to love its parents by feeling their love and returning it as they grow up. The day arrives when the child becomes an adult and helps their ageing parent to wash and dress.

The way to create an abundance of love is simple. Help is the key that unlocks the door to love. If you are doubtful, try loving someone without helping them. The opposite of help is harm and all actions originate from one of these two motives: either help or harm. If you are not loved, then check your motives and actions

To help is to love.
The more you help,
the more you love.

and see if they *really help* others. HELP, allows us to respond to other people's needs and to give them what *they* need. You may give or receive the most expensive gift, but if it is not really needed the experience will be devoid of love. In the same way, we perform actions that we *think* will help others and feel bitterly disappointed when people help us in ways we do not need. We can only learn to love and be loved by helping others with what they really *need.* As you learn to love in this way, there will come a point when your every thought and action will be guided by the wish to help. A human being who is motivated by helping becomes the master of love and life. They become a magnet, a beacon, a fountain and a force of love.

HELP is The Way to Reunite with God

As you begin to read these words, I want you to listen carefully to what you hear in your heart. By the time you have finished reading this sentence, millions of individuals will have performed some form of religious ritual. People perform religious rituals as habitually as they brush their teeth or go shopping, yet fellow human beings are crying out for help, next door, down the street and in cities world wide. Right now over two hundred million people are homeless. Nine hundred and forty-five million people will go hungry *today.* Can you hear anything yet? I can hear cries for help coming from all around me. Whenever you pray, meditate, chant, perform a religious ritual or go to your place of worship, listen carefully to what you hear.

A woman once came up to me on the street and asked me where I was going. I said, *"to help the homeless".* She then asked me, *"What is your religion?"* I paused for a moment and said, *"HELP."* She mocked, *"How can help be a religion?"* I moved on.

What can be more spiritual than a life devoted to helping others?

I believe that God lives in the hearts of everyone and helping reaches the heart of God. Help in its pure form is a completely harmless action which opens people's hearts and minds. I am certain that being spiritual is about saving people's lives and souls. HELP relieves suffering and saves lives and souls. Whatever our race or religion, I believe that above all God wants us to help each other. HELP leads to love, and love is felt in the heart, the dwelling place of God. All we need do to be reunited with God is *help*.

Help is the most immediate action of all and needs to be rendered now. To help means to act *now* and *the slightest delay* or hesitation will result in the loss of life and soul. Wouldn't you expect help if you were crying out for help? So why can't we hear and respond to the cries of others? What would happen if we could hear and act on these cries for help? It would mean a change in our lifestyle and daily routine. It would mean sharing or giving away everything we do not need and perhaps even a complete redirection of our life purpose. What stops people from helping is ignorance, apathy, fear, greed, and desire. It is often more desirable to turn a blind eye to these truths about ourselves rather than to face them and help people.

HELP brings us out and into the open where people need us.

I have seen many religious people who hide behind their beliefs and religious buildings and do nothing to help the needy. The next time you begin to perform a religious ritual or begin the journey to church try this: for once, change direction and go onto the street or to a place where you can help the needy. If today you are on the way to a bar, club, cinema or shop, change direction and go where you can help someone. You may feel lost the first few times, as our lives are conditioned to follow patterns and expectations, even in the *name* of God.

Many people devote their lives and soul to God by following the code of conduct set out by their religions. Religion and spirituality have become marketable commodities which we promote by logos, brand names, appealing rituals and ritualised appeals. This is why the major religious organisations have outgrown the largest multinationals and wield more power than most governments. These organisations get bigger and more powerful, but is that what is needed to reunite humanity with God? I think not, since devotees from one religion often compete or fight with another, just as nations do. The word religion means, 'a way to reunite with God'.

Help yourself and you will reach the heart of God.
Help an animal and you will reach the heart of God.
Help a human being and you will reach the heart of God.
Help the Earth and you will reach the heart of God.

HELP is The Way to Promote Social Change

The notion of social change can mean many things to many people. I am glad that it does. It is my intention to expose the extraordinary potential of HELP as the way to promote *any* form of social change. So regardless of whether you are a social worker seeking welfare reform, or a revolutionary secretly conspiring rebellion, you may be wise to consider HELP as a means of social change. Why?

HELP promotes the common good.

Social change is a very complex matter and involves many agendas such as, freedom, justice, peace, distribution of wealth and power, equal rights, etc. My definition of social change however is very simple: to promote the common good. Firstly I'd like to look back and see what we have learnt about social change.

A great deal has been said and written over the centuries, about the means of achieving social change. Many ways have been tried, yet the majority of our species continues to suffer. Is it possible that the various means we have been using to achieve social change are actually the cause of social strife? To date we have used *revolution* as a means to change social and political conditions. By revolution I mean both violent and nonviolent means of confrontation. Let me explain. Revolution by violent means was used in China to overthrow dynastic rule. Revolution by nonviolent means was used by the Indians to regain power from British rule.

I believe that any form of resistance, violent or passive is revolutionary, since they both confront an oppressor in order to promote social change. The use of nonviolence, though not as common, is as much a tool of revolution as violence, as when Gandhi led the rebellion against British rule of India. However, there is really no such thing as nonviolence where there is an intention to confront an oppressor. Confronting the oppressor will simply manifest a different form of violence. Ironically, the means of revolution, whether violent or nonviolent, are often used after the revolution as the means to dominate or deceive the masses into accepting continuing change in government and its rule.

For example, Gandhi used nonviolent means to defeat the British but even now, some five decades after the British have gone, the mass of India's population are still being oppressed by means of nonviolent government. In China, where violence was used to crush dynastic rule, successive governments have used violence as a means of government. In both cases the means of revolution, violent or nonviolent, did not benefit the masses. The sad thing is, in both countries the oppressed are as oppressed as they have been for centuries. I am not saying that we should rule out confrontation from the social change equation. No, but I think we should wise up and use the means not only to bring a change in power but in our long term capacity for helping the oppressed *as well*.

Revolution brings violence, disorder and disruption with little substantive change. Revolution, in its original form means, 'to revolve'. Revolution is triggered then by *action and reaction*, which leads to revolution and counter revolution and so on. A revolving nightmare for the oppressed masses.

Evolution signifies change that is peaceful, orderly and progressive. It is guided by *action and response*, based on evasion rather than confrontation. HELP is the key activity that makes evolution possible. It is a gradual or radical means of social change that takes the path of *nonresistance*.

I believe that HELP and helping each other is *the* most peaceful and effective way of promoting the common good. This is how it works. Those seeking social change use all their energy and resources to help each other. To confront the oppressor would be seen as a waste and hindrance to promoting *the common good*. For instance, the 'blacks' in the 'projects' or ghettos of the USA, instead of confronting 'the whites' could unite and mobilise *themselves*. The oppressor, who is in this instance 'the whites' would not be in the calculation. Black people would take their power by taking responsibility for helping each other. They would create their own employment, wealth, health, education and welfare systems.

Freedom comes from helping each other.

For thousands of years the poor have remained poor regardless of the change in power. Why? It is because they have never learnt to help themselves and each other. I have seen first hand, that when people help each other, progress in every area of society is maximised. One of the best examples of help promoting the common good is in The Maldives. With less than three hundred thousand people and very limited natural resources, The Maldives co-operate in running a country where there are no beggars, homeless or unemployed.

To the agents of social change wherever you are, I ask you to consider HELP as the means of uniting and mobilising your people to manifest the message of your prophets and social reformers. Do not wait for others to do it for you, because the only way to overcome your helpless condition is to help each other. HELP is the fastest and easiest way to promote lasting social change for *all* members of a society. That process begins with *one* person who is willing to give *all* to the cause. Look at the lives of Gandhi, Emily Pankhurst, Malcolm X and Steve Biko. How did they conduct themselves? What was their message for you? Their effort means nothing, if we do not act to realise what they came to do. The one thing common to all social reformers is that they come to *help* humanity and their message can only be made manifest through the universal medium of helping each other.

HELP is The Way To Promote Human Evolution

The discovery of HELP as a way of promoting evolutionary change will lead us into a quantum leap in human evolution. Yet, how can such a common activity like help be the key for unlocking *all* the doors to human evolution? Very simply, every species *helps* itself to survive, multiply, solve problems, overcome crisis and create new possibilities. That is evolution! Reflect for a moment on our species' history. During our evolution from knuckle-walkers to space-travellers, we have spent most of our time as hunter-gatherers living in groups. We chose to live in groups because we could help each other to survive and procreate.

HELP is at the heart of evolution.

Every species on the Earth has managed to survive as *a direct result* of being able to help themselves. Our species is one of the most fragile life forms on the Earth. The reason we have survived and evolved so far, is due to our limitless capacity to help ourselves.

*HELP is much more
than a solution
to a crisis.*

*HELP is a pathway
for limitless
creative potential.*

The more we have helped ourselves, the more we have developed in every facet of our existence: biologically, mentally, emotionally, and spiritually. If you look back at your own life for example, you will see how much help you have received from your family, friends, teachers, preachers, police, and public services, so that you could *evolve* from conception to your current state of well-being.

Through helping ourselves, each one of us evolves every day, and combined, we all promote the evolution of our species over the ages. HELP has been *the* pathway for our evolution from the beginning, not only for humans, but for all species. As a whole, the question is: how does The HELP Process actually promote human evolution? This is how. When people help each other we make progress, which in turn promotes evolutionary change. My understanding of human evolution is *any progress that promotes the common good.* Progress and human evolution are intimately connected and, though definitions may vary, the one common factor is that HELP promotes progress in every area of human existence. My equation for human evolution is:

Help = Progress = Evolution

So far in the evolutionary journey of our species, we have used help instinctively to evolve. In order to take a quantum leap in our evolution, we need to become aware of the greater potential of The HELP Process and consciously evolve. By becoming aware of this equation, we can consciously guide our evolutionary journey.

Our immediate evolutionary aim is to help humanity evolve from hunter-hunted to helper-helped. The HELP Process can be used on many levels to further this transformation. To demonstrate the power of help, I would like you to choose a situation, condition or arena, on any level from personal to global. For the sake of explanation, I have chosen two cases which I would like you to compare and adapt to your own.

The first case is actual and uses The HELP Process as a solution for starvation. In 1985 the Live Aid concert was held, in which musicians performed in order to raise funds to feed the starving people of Ethiopia. This phenomenal event was motivated and made possible by people helping each other.

The second case is an idea of how we can use The HELP Process to promote the well being of humanity. Millions of individuals are suffering and dying as a result of having contracted an immune deficiency called A.I.D.S. Hundreds of pharmaceutical companies are competing with each other to be the first to find the cure for A.I.D.S. Why? To ensure long term financial gains. What would happen if all these companies came together to find the cure, albeit to split the profits? Is it possible that the cure for A.I.D.S. exists now, but in fragmented pieces in separate laboratories? So much *progress* can be made if they share information and results from existing experiments, resources, and moral support.

The idea of the world's pharmaceutical giants helping each other, for the sake of saving human life, may sound far fetched now, but necessity will soon demand such a unified process of co-operation. In the same way, we can approach the crisis in the human condition as a challenge to be overcome via co-operation. That may be, but the crisis is becoming worse and may reach a point of inertia. So why don't people act?

Most people do not act to change worsening conditions until they become life threatening *for them.* It is then that they mobilise everything to put things right. It is only a matter of time before all of us are facing life threatening situations *every day* that could kill us. Then it will be, *'enough is enough'*! At this point in our evolutionary journey a completely new phenomenon in human behaviour will take place on a grand scale. *A fundamental shift from competition to co-operation* will take place as individuals work out that co-operation is by far the most effective means of existence. Things will get much worse, however, before people wake up.

In our evolutionary journey, we are at the stage of *the darkness before the dawn.* As the swirling mass of humanity sleeps however, some people are beginning to wake up to the new way. I believe that by the early part of the 21st century there will be an initial critical mass of 120 million people who will start the process of a world evolution.

We are on the eve of a world evolution.

Whilst the majority of humanity continues to compete, the silent ranks of a new species, whose consciousness is grounded in co-operation, is multiplying. I am certain that there are millions of individuals and groups who are trying, in their own way, to move from competition to co-operation. Others are motivated to help, but lack the method to manifest their intent.

Helping each individual move or shift from hunter to helper is *the most dynamic way to promote human evolution.* The whole project or process of human evolution hinges on the capacity of individuals and groups to understand and actively use The HELP Process. Each one of us is like a carrier of a very powerful tool – HELP. It can be used in every situation and condition. HELP *is* the key activity that will unlock all the doors to human evolution and serve as a solution to our crisis. The more we help each other, the more we shall overcome our difficulties and take a quantum leap in human evolution.

The idea of creating a quantum leap in human evolution can be overwhelming, especially if you intend to participate in making it happen. I hope the following explanation helps you to see how HELP will work in the big picture and the process leading to that point. The process of creating a quantum leap in human evolution will necessitate the following:

First: A need which will then provoke a response. That need is a crisis within our species.

Second: A solution must be ready if we are to respond effectively. That solution, is The HELP Process and people helping each other. (See *Participation*, page 261)

Third: To diffuse the solution to other individuals. That is being done *right now*. This is how the process works, on the ground.

A quantum leap in evolution begins with a precondition, in this case a crisis, which necessitates such a leap. One individual, or a few, pioneer and pave the way by finding a new approach or solution to the crisis. One by one, more of the species then become aware of the benefits and pick up the tools of transformation. In this way, the solution is spread from one to another until it reaches a first critical mass. This process accelerates as the numbers increase from one critical mass to another, until an ultimate critical mass is reached. At this point a quantum leap in evolution occurs, where the application of the solution spreads throughout the species at lightning speeds.

The above process of promoting human evolution has already been activated. Your participation is needed to reach an initial critical mass. The HELP Process is a practical method that enables and empowers an individual to move from competition to co-operation. I believe that HELP is the way to promote human evolution. The HELP Process is the solution. Whichever way we approach our crisis, The HELP Process will play a pivotal part in promoting human evolution.

HELP is unique.

Helping each other is very practical, spiritual and simple. Whatever capacity you have can be used to help those overwhelmed by sorrow, those bereft of wealth and those stricken by suffering. Helping is a very powerful and unique action. Every time you help another person, plant or animal, you create *love*, a vibration in your surroundings, which then reflects outward and around the world. Even the *smallest* action of help does this!

The act of help is holy. It is pure love. On a sunny day, I was watching some children play. A little girl came off the swing in the playground, out came the cry as she fell. We rushed to help her. She had grazed her knee. A boy who was waiting to get on the swing, peeled a plaster from his leg and stuck it on her knee. This boy's simple action of help is as mighty as walking on the moon or becoming enlightened. Can you feel the power of this simple action? Imagine what kind of world it would be if we all helped each other in such simple ways? Now I would like to conclude my response to the question, 'What is help?'

HELP is a unique activity because it unites matter and spirit into one. A thought or action of help is an *activity* that is free from the anticipation of the fruits of action. HELP has a deep cosmic significance, in that it is supported by the very process of evolution. If we are held by the fruits of our actions, then our sole concerns are centred on the material plane of life. To help is to see higher than action and its fruits, into the Divine. This elevates the action into the spiritual plane of life, on which *the process of evolution* is based. HELP is a universal symbol of evolution. Every species helps itself to evolve.

The
Way
of
HELP

HELP as a Way of Life

Many people are searching for a new way of life, but what are they looking for? Since we look for that which we have lost or need, the search is for what is missing in our lives. People are looking for a way of life that will help them fulfil their needs and guide them in times of uncertainty. Life is a journey and we need *a way to live* because without a way we get lost. A way of life is the greatest fortune we can find, as it brings to us everything we need.

I believe that a way of life should serve *all* your needs as you grow physically and spiritually. Should it not? Your way of life may be based on a spiritual doctrine, ancient prophecy, or mythological or scientific principles. The question is: does your way of life serve *all* your needs? Over the past forty thousand years many ways of existence have been invented by 'man'. Their one common aim, is to help the practitioner. Today, there are hundreds of different ways of life, from sun worship to scientific laws. They are all trying to do one thing – help.

What will The Way of HELP do for you?

- *Help you when you are alone, desperate and in impossible situations.*

- *HELP will bring peace, ease, prosperity and joy to you and your family.*

- *HELP will meet all your needs and bless you with the love, power, wisdom and the grace of God.*

If you already have a religion or belief system, then HELP will play a central role in its practice. The Way of HELP will help you to get from *here to there* – wherever there is for *you*. That is why help is central to *all* races, religions and belief systems.

To demonstrate the role of help in religion I am going to use examples from the Christian tradition. In a key biblical event, when the Israelites were in need of water, God asked Moses to strike a rock and water flowed from it. This rock was handed down through generations to Jacob, who used it as a 'Pillar Stone' to build the 'House of God'. The bible refers to this stone as:

The Stone of Help

The Stone of Help is symbolic of God's work. The rock represents the foundations of life and the water signifies the source. The Stone is witness to God's promise from Moses and Joshua to Abraham, Isaac and Jacob. The 'Stone of Help', also called the 'Stone of Destiny', *lia-fáil,* was used to ordain kings and is said to be connected to Peter, whom Jesus called the rock on which he would build his church*.

The Stone of Help is the greatest gift God gave to the Church of Christ because it represents the work of God throughout many thousands of years. The Stone is about the salvation of the entire world and that is why help has played a central role in all religions. It will bring peace and prosperity to all nations far beyond human comprehension. Christians believe that when Jesus returns he will sit upon The Stone of Help as 'King of Kings' and 'Lord of Lords'. Is it a coincidence that the name Jesus means in Hebrew 'he who helps'?

The Stone of Help represents the Global Church of God.

But where is the stone now? During the middle ages the stone was carried for safe keeping, first to Scotland, then Ireland, to England in Westminster Abbey and now rests in Edinburgh Castle. The Coronation Chair is built around it, with a sign beside it

* See Matthew 16:18.

labelled: *Jacob's Pillar Stone (Genesis 28:18)*. But is this the real Stone of Help?

For over 25 centuries, the kings of Israel, Ireland, Scotland and England, including the present Queen, Elizabeth II, have been crowned on that stone. No other nation in history has had a coronation stone like the United Kingdom. The central message of The Stone of Help is about God helping humanity so that we can help ourselves. *HELP is the cornerstone of God's house on Earth.*

All religions are trying to save humanity and the Earth. But how? With God's help! The Way of HELP is like a rope which runs through the heart of all races and religions, tying them into *one work of God.* There is *one God* and HELP is a unifying force that unites *all* people. Because help unites all people, it is central to God's work for the salvation of humanity.

The Way of HELP is unique because anyone from any persuasion can practise it to manifest God's help. HELP is an interaction, not a religion or organisation that you join or follow. The *Way* of HELP is a *life-force* that flows from the heart of God and moves from person to person via helpful actions. Look how The Way of HELP has reached you without you having to become a devotee, disciple or follower. Since help flows directly from the heart of God, the helping hand of God will protect, guide and help you directly – now.

HELP is the hand of God

Do not be afraid – I am with you!
I am your God – let nothing terrify you!
I will make you strong and help you.
I will protect you.
Those who are angry with you
will know the shame of defeat.
Those who fight against you will die,
and will disappear from the Earth.
I am the Lord your God.
I strengthen you and say;
Do not be afraid; I will help you.   ISAIAH 41: 10-13

65

The Way of HELP is the way to experience the power of God. To demonstrate the power of the helping hand of God, I am going to use the parable of Noah's Ark and the flood. In the story, God asked Noah to build an Ark to save humanity and the animals from the flood. When God asked Noah he was forty years of age. No one believed in Noah's Ark or helped him, but as the Ark was central to the salvation of humanity, God's work, *one man* with the help of God completed the supernatural task. The hand of God, helped Noah to build the Ark, load the animals, weather the storms and the flood to arrive safely on dry land.

Why was Noah, a common man, anointed to do God's central work? God chose Noah because he was humble and available to work for God. There are two kinds of work. You work for yourself or you work for God. You have to choose either to work for your own greed and glory or to work for God, by being humble and available. Many spiritual people help to do God's work as long as they get the glory. The Way of HELP is a way of life *devoted* to helping *selflessly* to do God's central work on Earth.

The Way of HELP is a way to help people with your God given gift. Imagine what *you* can create with God's help? For example, God has asked me to *help* create a world living in peace and ease – Paradise. Looking at the condition of the world, such a task seems impossible and yet The Way of HELP is flourishing. HELP as a way of life, is a way of helping to do God's central work. *Ask God how you can help*. When God asks me to do something, I know it shall be done. God is my helper and provider.

The Way of HELP is a way for God to help you. When I have felt alone, desperate and in impossible situations, God has helped me in ways beyond my imagination. How can you manifest God's help onto yourself? Ask! Say, *"God help me."* Then do what God asks of you. For instance, when you are ill, you seek the help of a doctor and to get well you do what is asked. If you want God's help, then you need to seek God and do what is asked of you.

When you seek God's help and live accordingly, the supernatural will manifest in your life. During one moment of desperation, God told me, *"As long as you remain devoted to The Way of HELP, everything I have asked you to do will happen,"* and so it has. If you help to do God's work, then God will help you. When this happens, one person is enough, more than enough, to complete what millions find impossible. One person who is *devoted* to doing God's work will manifest the supernatural with ease. In this way, one person can help an entire race, religion and nation.

The power of one with God's help.

Have you ever wondered why the world is in such a poor condition despite all the religious organisations and their followers? Why are so many spiritual people poor and powerless to take authority? Millions of people are stressed, depressed, heavy, busy, burdened and burnt out. Why? Because they have *blocked* the flow of help into their lives. The Way of HELP makes our lives easier, lighter, loving, playful, powerful and joyful.

You do not have to live like others or take what society gives you and wish 'if only'. HELP is a Way of Life that makes 'if' into 'so'. Look, my life *is* paradise. I am one of the most blessed men that has walked the Earth. How is this? How can a common man without a religious bone in his body, be blessed with a life of paradise? God's help comes to me in the form of blessings. What are blessings? God's help! Every time I *give* and *receive* help, I am being blessed by God. So, the more you use HELP as a way of life, the more your life will be blessed by God. Simple!

When there is a *lack* of peace , ease, prosperity and joy in your life, find out where the flow of help is being obstructed or wasted. Do not block the flow of help. A person, organisation or nation that obstructs The Way of HELP, will bring destruction on themselves. HELP is the way God blesses our lives and when we stop the flow of help, we suffer and die. You may think what I am saying is too simple. It is very simple. Do you know why all the rulers and their empires were destroyed, including Hitler and the Third Reich?

Hitler said, *"Never believe in help from the outside;*
Never believe in help from other nations."

Hitler blocked the flow of God's help from reaching the German people. *All* the suffering and destruction in humanity is caused by something or someone obstructing The Way of HELP. Ironically, some of the world's biggest religious organisations and their followers are not aware of the way to regulate the flow of God's help to humanity. This may be difficult to face, but why are there over one billion believers in God living in *abject* poverty? The *leader* of a religious organisation is in the position to open or close the flow of God's help to the people.

I believe the reason for the poverty in the world's religions is that their leaders do not know how to manifest God's help for themselves, let alone their people. Why else? The Way of HELP will change this by showing you and your people the way to practise HELP as a way of life. All it takes is for one person to bring God's helping hand down to humanity. As in the story of Noah, one person can promote the healing and salvation of humanity by the HELP of God. You may *think* that it is impossible for one person to do so much, and it is, if you try to do it yourself. Put aside *your* limitations and imagine what can become of humanity and the Earth with God's helping hand. That is why HELP is the salvation to our crisis and the way to create Paradise on Earth.

Many people have visions and dreams, but do not have the resources to manifest them. Why? Ignorance of God as the source of resources. God is the source of help that flows *directly* and *indirectly* from person to person. The moment you *ask* or *offer* to help, you activate the source of resources. Once you affirm The Way of HELP with your whole being, every helpful action will come back to you many fold, in the form of blessings. In this way HELP will meet *all* your needs and bless you with the love, power, wisdom and grace of God.

> ***HELP is the harbinger of all***
> ***that you need, want and wish.***

The Way of HELP is a very pure and simple way of life without rituals, laws, chronicles, prophets, priests, churches and hierarchy. Although HELP is a very powerful way of life, it is easy to practise. You begin by helping yourself, albeit to feed your body and soul. Think about it. Can you name one need which cannot be fulfilled with help? What other way of life can serve you like HELP?

HELP as a way of life is very important, because the way you live your life affects the whole of humanity. Each human being is like a cell in the body of humanity and *your* way of life either *helps* or *harms* the whole body. By helping yourself, you help the human species. To help one person is to help every living being.

The Way of HELP works for all people of any race, religion, condition or consciousness because the interaction of help is governed by a *universal* process. As you put The HELP Process into practice, you will begin to experience help not as an isolated or sporadic event, but a continuous *flow of helpful actions*. Your mind and body will become accustomed to the 'Way of HELP' as the easiest and most natural way of being in the world. HELP will have become a way of life.

The Foundations of HELP

The Way of HELP is a way of life rooted *in* life. HELP is the root of the tree of life and the more we help ourselves, the more we live life to the full. The Way of HELP harbours unlimited potential, but how can we use this awesome power – consciously? Where do we start? Since The Way of HELP is rooted in life, we begin to use help by focusing on the very foundations of our lives. The word foundation means corner stone, origin, source, support or a place to stand on.

What are the foundations of a human being?

Just as a tree needs healthy roots to grow, a human being needs strong foundations to live and evolve. We know that a tree needs strong roots to survive the change of seasons, and so a human being needs to have deep rooted foundations to *withstand* changes and challenges. Common sense tells us that what we stand upon determines our stability, but what are the foundations upon which to build our lives? When we look *closely* at the lives of our parents, teachers, preachers and politicians, we often see unhappy, unstable, weak and wrecked lives. Why? Are there a *common* set of foundations that support human existence and if so, what are they?

The foundations of a human being are: *Health, Home, Family* and *Work*. These are the four sources which sustain the human life support system. They are the foundations upon which your life and future are built. The neglect of any *one* of these foundations is the cause of the dis-ease and destruction of many, many lives. At first glance, these foundations appear simple and even obvious. Indeed they are *fundamental*. But, did you know what they are and why they are not taught or talked about in our homes, schools, churches and society?

70

Do not underestimate the importance of these foundations, for they are the *life source* of human existence. If you look back at the lives of your parents and grandparents, you will see how much the condition of their Health, Home, Family and Work determined their *destiny*.

Health, Home, Family and Work are the wells of human life. They promote your welfare. Although a human being has countless needs, *all* of them are fulfilled by nurturing these four foundations. In turn, whatever you want to make of your life, it will depend upon the condition of these foundations. Think about it. Where else is your source of power and prosperity going to come from? The Foundations of HELP are the *wells* of your *welfare* and the wells of human salvation.

The Foundations of HELP

These foundations will determine your faith and future.

When your foundations are weak, you will feel unstable, tired and weakened in faith. Although our faith is not supposed to depend on anything but God, faith comes with a shovel and we need physical strength. Faith needs *energy* which comes from these foundations. Strong foundations mean strong faith.

The weaker your foundations are, the less energy, power and faith you will have to accomplish your goal. When all four of our foundations are weak, we become helpless. I know this to be true as there was a time in my life when being homeless, poor in health and without a family and work weakened my faith to its lowest point. When our faith is weakened or broken, we are open to all kinds of negative influences. Desperate people do desperate things such as crime, drugs, prostitution, corruption, adultery, which all originate from weak foundations and weakened faith.

Most people feel weak in some foundations, but ignore the signs until their life and faith fall apart. Ironically, the leaders of countries are the most prone to collapse in their faith due to the pressure. Wise up and act now. By nurturing these foundations you will build a life based on strong faith. Health, Home, Family and Work are your *real riches*, and the more you nurture them the richer and more powerful you will become.

To begin the practice of HELP as a way of life, we must first nurture its foundations in our own lives. Health, Home, Family and Work are The Foundations of HELP because they promote Human Evolution and Life Procreation. Can you think of a single interaction or situation which does not *depend* on them? They are The Foundations of HELP because they *help* our species in every arena of its existence.

Looking at the crisis in humanity, we can see how our species has neglected to develop these foundations and why the whole world culture is falling apart. Our species has erected lofty buildings, created complex cultures and high ideals, but the very foundations that support human existence are rotten. Our cities look very rosy from the top of the edifice, but there is a stench of rot under the surface.

Everything created and built that does not serve these foundations will fall. As we build for the future, let us focus on what will serve and pass this wisdom to the generations which follow. Each one of us must understand that the foundations of our individual lives support those of our family and our community. We depend on each other and future generations depend on what we build. It is that simple.

The Foundation of Health

We start with the development of Health, because we carry our health with us. The current state of our health determines our actions and mirrors the quality of our lives. The current condition of our health is the story of how we have lived. From that perspective, it is easy to understand that how we live now determines our future health. Most people take their health for granted and neglect their natural needs. This neglect is fostered by misplaced priorities, as people often take better care of their household pets, their cars and clothes than their own health.

We tend to think that we are healthy but, when we look closely, we can feel the aches and pains in our body, anxiety and worry in our emotions and the lack of peace in our minds. The word *health* comes from the Greek word 'holos' meaning 'whole'. The whole person needs to be nurtured in order to be healthy.

In the big picture, if we look at the condition of other life forms on the Earth, humans appear to be the most unhealthy and diseased. The health of our species is becoming worse. With the advent of high speed travel, every illness from the common cold to complex diseases can be transmitted across the world within hours. What is more, the nature of disease, from sore throats to A.I.D.S., through rape and child abuse, to crime and corruption of all kinds, is a physical manifestation of social disease.

These diseases are breaking down human nature. People are becoming paranoid, about where they live, what they eat, how they travel, and the safety of their children at school and on the street. All these afflictions are rotting humanity's foundations of health. Accordingly, as humans are part of the ecology system, we are infecting vegetation and wildlife with our pollutant waste and erratic behaviour. The root cause of the worsening condition of the Earth is due to our own sickness. The Earth is getting sick, because we, its stewards, are sick.

The way to restore your own health, humanity's and the Earth's, is very simple. Nurture your foundation of health by learning to listen to your natural needs and make their fulfilment your priority in life. By creating new priorities based on your *natural* needs, you will naturally develop new habits which will help you to develop your foundation of health. Just as a diseased person infects others, a human being who is in a healthy condition sends out a vibration which affects everyone around them.

The Foundation of Home

A home is a refuge, a place to rest and recover. It is a place where we feel at peace and ease. *Home* is also a sacred place and referred to as a 'temple' or 'the house of God'. Home represents the centre of one's life and family. That is why we say, *'home is where the heart is'*. Almost every creature has a place to which it returns at the end of the day. Home is where we feel a sense of belonging and run to in times of trouble and ill health, a place to come to after long journeys and in which to celebrate birthdays, marriages and thanksgiving. In turn, the condition of our Home has a direct impact on our Health, Family life and Work. The way we live at home has a profound effect on the way we conduct our affairs in the outside world. A home that does not serve your needs, will drain your energy before you leave the front door. In order to be effective in the world, you will need a place to 'rest your head'. What kind of a home do you have?

Take a walk into a rich or poor area of a big city. You will smell and hear air and noise pollution, and see box-like homes filled with electric cables and concrete gardens. You will find people living in isolation behind locked doors, not knowing the names of their neighbours let alone loving them. Does any of this ring true in your life? For many millions who are homeless, the situation is desperate, and the numbers of homeless are rising worldwide. Millions more live in poor housing, ghettos and shanty towns. Having been homeless myself, I know that the absence of a decent home destroys the heart and soul of a human being. Perhaps the presidents of our nations should spend a week on the streets to realise the need for proper housing. As the human population increases, land has become more scarce and expensive. People who are poor are forced to live in ghettos, which by their very nature breed disease, crime, corruption, prostitution, segregation and ultimately anarchy. Sooner or later, these problems find their way into our homes whether we are rich or poor. Ironically, that's what we mean by the phrase, 'the chickens have come *home* to roost'.

Whatever is coming back into your life has its origins in your home, since that is where you conduct your inner life which manifests in the outer world. Often, what is discussed in the living room, bedroom or on the dining table, is what happens in your life. Whether we live in a cardboard box, a hut, a house, mansion or palace, we have to understand that it is not the type of home we live in, but how homely it is that makes us feel at home. How we feel at home then, affects our conduct in society.

The Foundation of Family

Our family is the primary source of help and love. At the moment of birth, we were helpless and depended on our parents to help us survive those critical years. These formative years with our family are the foundation upon which our lives are built. Our whole life style, what we eat, the clothes we wear, where we live, the work we do and the way we raise our children, is deeply connected to those early years. If that is true, then the family we are born and raised in determines who we become. Does that mean that we are destined to live and die according to the way we were raised by our family? No, because we have the free will to change the way we think and behave.

As we exercise our free will, we realise that a family does not necessarily mean blood ties, but can be those we love, trust and work with. We need such people to feel a sense of belonging, and even if they do not live with us, just to know that they are there for us is enough.

Over the past few hundred years, *the family* has undergone many changes with many people living far away from their families. People living lonely lives often join movements, cults and clubs in search of intimacy, but the intimacy of family life cannot be found in these institutions. What people are looking for is deeply fulfilling, loving relationships with a spouse, offspring, parents and grandparents. Nothing can replace the love and joy which can be found in a close knit family. Having lost my own parents at a young age, I know how it feels to be without a family.

In our family we feel intimacy, kindness, compassion, joy, and unity which spirals outward into society and humanity. The family is the centre of humanity and, without a central focus, we become disoriented, lost and lonely. Loneliness is one of the major causes of depression in the modern era, and in the last century cases of depression have doubled with every generation. Why?

Where do you belong?

Human existence has become too separate and impersonal for the individual to feel affinity with fellow human beings. When I say hello to people in the street, on a train, or in the park, I get all kinds of reactions. When we were children, the most important thing in our lives was our family. As we became adults, that priority was misplaced and replaced with other 'important things'. We have to realise that a family is our source of love. We cannot do without it.

The Foundation of Work

Most people have a love-hate relationship with their work. People who dislike their work, go to work in order to earn money and pay for what they need. We tend to think that work is not an activity which we should love and enjoy. That is why people see their work as a burden they carry like an unwilling donkey. Work is a way to fulfil our destiny and needs to be connected to what we believe in. Each one of us has something unique to contribute.

When we work towards our vision, we are building the foundation of work which stands with and supports our health, home and family in more ways than money can. Working towards what we love is a demonstration of faith, which brings us much more than working for money. Faith is the source of our future, which can be anything we desire. When we work with faith we build the foundation of our future. It does not matter what kind of work we do, as long as it gives us the feeling of having done something meaningful.

Everyday, millions of people go to work, but what are they working for? Surely not all of them are desperate to provide for themselves and their families? Most people go to work like sheep, following the one in front without vision. They have lost their own sense of direction and like sheep, they are herded by their leaders, who in turn are controlled by the shareholders of that company. This is called *exploitation* and as the pressure for more profit increases, companies relocate in third world countries where land and labour are cheap.

A business man once told me, *"when I go to work, I go to war."* We may not be waging war with weapons, but we are waging war with our work. For example, when a speculator makes a 'killing' on the commodities market, somewhere in the world, ordinary working people receive a devastating blow. Land is raped and wild life destroyed. The next time you hear of a company announce record profits, reflect on the cost in human suffering to workers and their families. The work we do affects not only our own family, but also humanity and the Earth.

We have to choose the work we do with honesty and integrity. Remaining true to what we believe in is the greatest reward our work can bring. Work is about devotion to a way of helping others, not exploitation. Working to help others is the ultimate contribution we can make to the family of humanity. How different would our world be if our life's work was focused on helping others?

The Foundations of HELP are Rooted in Life

When I tell people that my life is paradise, they often don't believe me. What is the secret of making life paradise? Very simple. Peace and ease. Make your Health, Home, Family and Work your focus in life, as these are the foundations of life that will bring you peace and ease – Paradise. This is how it works. Place your ear to these foundations and listen to the *natural* needs coming from deep down, then devote yourself to nurturing your natural needs.

The more you nurture these foundations, the more at peace and ease your life will become. A lot of spiritual people believe that one's peace should depend solely on faith. This is a myth. Why? Millions of people pray, meditate, chant, practise rituals and use substances to feel at peace but, without ease, peace will always be a struggle and short lived. Your Health, Home, Family and Work nurture your physical and spiritual needs, bringing ease to your body and peace to your mind.

The only way to experience *real* and *lasting* peace and ease is by focusing your way of life towards nurturing your Health, Home, Family and Work. What is your way of life focused on? Where are you going and what are you building on? Just as the roots of a tree determine its condition, these foundations determine the condition of your life, who you are, and what you have become. Our species has created and built so much, but so many lives are broken because we have neglected to nurture the very foundations of being human. Is it any wonder that we do not have a world living in peace and ease?

As we delve deeper, we become aware that the foundations of a human being are also the foundations of human kind. This means the condition of these foundations in your life determines the condition of humanity. Common sense will now tell you that the way to help create a whole world at peace is by mending our own lives. What use are the peace movements, the demonstrations and prizes of such struggles when our lives remain in turmoil? How can we build the 'kingdom of Heaven on Earth' when the foundations of our lives are broken?

Yearning for these ideals is universal, but we have to understand that the only way humanity will manifest them is by establishing its foundations: The Foundations of Human Evolution and Life Procreation. How can we do this? On the individual level, we can first focus on our own foundations and having done so help others. On the collective level, we can talk about them with our children and teach them in schools. We can enlighten our political and spiritual leaders so that the development of these foundations become part of their manifestos. When your leaders place The Foundations of HELP: Health, Home, Family and Work at the top of their agendas, you and your country will prosper in every way imaginable.

The Pan Pathways

In The *Foundations of HELP*, I said that The Way of HELP was a way of life rooted in life. Now I am going to reveal how The Way of HELP flows from the very source of life. A *Way* is a 'path-to-be-followed' in order to get from here to there. The Way of HELP is the pathway leading to the very source of life, God.

HELP flows from the heart of God.

The Way of HELP is a life-force that flows from the heart of God and sustains all life. All our lives are woven together by HELP. Each one of us helps one another as a part of creation, just as our arms, hands, feet, legs and senses co-operate in sustaining the body. In the same way, every living being is continually helping another living being knowingly or unknowingly. One animal helps another, you help your friend, a mother helps her child, and the Earth helps to sustain all life forms.

HELP is the *high way* of life. HELP is one activity that is common to all forms of life. Why? God is the source of life and that is why every living being is *born* with the idea of HELP. The cry of a new born baby is a cry for help. Help is the most primal activity, for without help we suffer and die. The *whole* of creation depends upon HELP, *because* help flows from the source of life, God.

The Way of HELP is a whole, a total *way*, ordained by God for us to conduct our lives, in order to live the highest way of life. The Way of HELP is a practical and spiritual way to live and realise the Divine Will.

- **How does The Way of HELP work for you?**
- **Why is The Way of HELP a universal phenomenon?**

I shall demonstrate the unique potential of The Way of HELP, by responding to these questions. Many people and prophets in our past have revealed laws, prophecies and parables, but The Way of HELP originates from the very source of life. Now, the 'way' for a genuine seeker 'is here', for God has ordained a Way-to-be-followed.

How does The Way of HELP work for you?

The Way of HELP will help you in every situation and action for the rest of your life. You see, from the moment of your birth you have been using the activity of HELP to help yourself grow, and become who you are now. Common sense will then tell you that the more you know how to help yourself, the more you can make of your life, but how can we help ourselves more? Is HELP an activity or process which we can learn to master like a language or driving a car? Yes, and this is how it works. Every action we perform is an attempt to help ourselves. All actions are in turn governed by a process. By knowing how The HELP Process works, we can help ourselves much more in *every* interaction and situation.

Although human beings use help much more than other creatures, our species has yet to discover the super-potential of HELP. We have to understand that the idea of HELP is inherent in every action and, by discovering the process which governs all ideas and action, we become masters of The Way of HELP. The practice of HELP and the mastery of action are one. Both are governed by one process. But how does the process of action in HELP actually work, and how does one human being help another?

The activity of help begins with an idea and ends with action. Between these two *points of activity,* exist what I call ***The Pan Pathways*** and the process of HELP works via four pathways: *Being, Knowing, Relating and Creating.* As I explain the workings of these pathways you will notice that they are in the present tense, i.e. Being, Knowing, Relating and Creating. This is because *everything* is alive and imbued with these pathways, which flow from one to another. When we use these pathways, they become channels that link us together via interaction. All our needs are met by being connected to other living beings and the Earth. A tree, fish, animal, insect and human being all use these pathways to live and procreate. Our world is governed by these pathways.

Your existence is governed by *Knowing* how to breathe, *Relating* to other human beings and the elements and *Creating* what you need to ensure *Being* in the world. *All* living beings use these pathways *all the time* to exist and give birth to new beings.

You and I came into being because our parents used their instinctive *Knowing* to have sexual intercourse by *Relating* to each other and *Creating* a new born *Being*. All acts of creation are governed in the same way by these pathways. I would now like to explain the actual practical function of The Pan Pathways, so you know how they work in practice. It is most important that you do not just believe, but that you *understand* and use these pathways consciously. As I introduce their practical application, I want to focus on the transfer of understanding to you so that you become actively involved in improving your actual condition.

Choose any activity, event, condition or object you want to bring into being and write it in the middle of the triangle, on the next page. Choose freely, since The Pan Pathways are universal this can be anything that comes to mind. Use your imagination, for it doesn't matter whether you choose the form or formless. My purpose is to demonstrate that The Pan Pathways govern any reality or existence you choose. Whatever you have chosen has come into *Being* via the interplay of *Knowing, Relating,* and *Creating.* Every process of creation begins and ends with *Being.* Look at how a clay pot is made. From our Being we use The Pathway of Knowing to spin the wheel, followed by The Pathway of Relating to the clay and using skills via The Pathway of Creating, a clay pot is brought into being. If you doubt what I am saying, do your utmost to cancel out any of these pathways that will not be present in the process of manifesting whatever you have chosen. Also, try to add more pathways that you deem necessary to the process.

When you want to change a situation or create something new, make a new triangle and write the aim in the centre. Then begin to use the four pathways starting from Being. I want you to start from your being, because all ideas and actions begin and end with being. Follow closely the chain of events of any action you perform and you will find that it originates from your Being and moves via Knowing, Relating and Creating to a new condition of Being. Being therefore is the centre and the source of our actions. That is why you write what you want to bring into *being,* in the centre of the triangle, which is also symbolic of *your Being.*

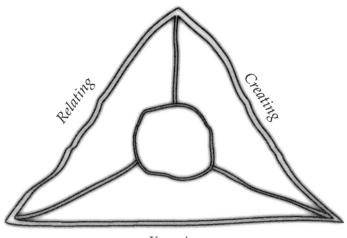

Knowing

Whatever it is that you want to create
you will have to use The Pan Pathways.

The Pan Pathways will change the way we create and enable you to manifest realities beyond your imagination. A new dawn in human creation has begun.

Creation is
woven together
by The
Pan Pathways.

This is how The Pan Pathways work. From your Being you are now interacting with the outside world via the Pathways of Knowing, Relating, and Creating. By being aware of how to use Knowing, Relating and Creating, you can change and create whatever you wish. Look closely at how you use these pathways to act, interact, create and exist in the world.

How are you interacting with everything that surrounds you? You are being sustained by your interaction with atoms, microbes, elements and the energy that surrounds you. The Pan Pathways are the means that make our interaction possible. These pathways are like invisible channels through which energy flows from one person to another and from one object-identity to another. They connect

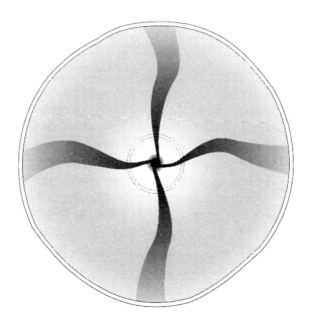

The Pan Pathways are used by all living beings.

everything – the whole of existence into one. This is why I have called them The Pan Pathways. The word Pan means 'one complete whole'. The symbol ⊙ represents 'one and infinity'.

Why is The Way of HELP a universal phenomenon?

The pathways of Being, Knowing, Relating and Creating flow across the whole of creation, interacting and connecting all realities of existence. The whole of creation exists through their interaction and without them creation would cease to exist. In fact each of the billions of living things on the Earth use them to stay alive and procreate. That means The Pan Pathways of Being, Knowing, Relating and Creating emanate from every living being in creation, so the question is: did creation come into being? If the answer is yes, then creation was also created via The Pan Pathways. If all acts of creation are governed by these pathways, then The Creator used the pathways of Being, Knowing, Relating and Creating to create creation.

In almost all religious traditions it is said that The Creator or God is omnipresent. The question is how? To say God, love, light or consciousness is not the answer. We want to know the *way God moves from one to another and still remains connected to all*. All living beings interact via the pathways of Being, Knowing, Relating and Creating. As each interaction begins and ends with Being, all interaction begins and ends with The Infinite Being. My understanding of what is called God or The Creator is what I call The Infinite Being, the centre of existence. Just as one's own being is the centre and source of existence, The Infinite Being is the centre of creation.

Because creation is connected via these pathways,
God moves and controls creation via the same pathways.

By the centre of existence I mean the heart of everything. Look how these pathways are now flowing from my being to your being.

In the same way, when we look at the big picture, all interaction from one being to another begins and ends with The Infinite Being. The Infinite Being is in this way omnipresent in every object, identity and action. Each one of us is therefore in continuous relationship with The Infinite Being. Unfortunately, humans in their present state of evolution are not fully aware of that eternal connection. We have to understand that God, The Infinite Being, lives in the heart of *every* being. The Way of HELP was set in

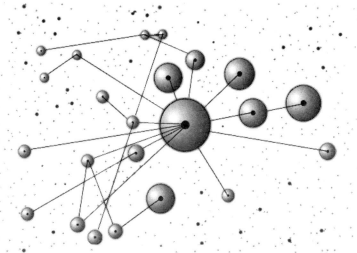

The Pan Pathways are Being, Knowing, Relating and Creating; these are the four Pathways that God uses to create creation.

motion from the dawn of creation. God created creation via the pathways of Being, Knowing, Relating and Creating. HELP flows from the heart of God and these pathways *carry* the life-force from the source of life to all creatures.

Without these pathways we cannot help ourselves and without help we cannot exist. HELP is the prime motive behind existence, creation and the constant activity of all beings *including* The Infinite Being. Helping is the eternal function of all beings in their relationship with The Eternal Infinite Being. By eternal I mean, 'without beginning and without end'. HELP is an eternal activity which spans the whole of creation through The Pan Pathways. HELP is therefore a universal phenomenon. This is not a sectarian idea, meant to replace religion and other belief systems. No, The Way of HELP is natural, primal and has *always* existed from the beginning. There is no exception to helping in creation. The Way of HELP is the way of creation, not a sectarian doctrine or organised religion. HELP is a way of existence in that it is used in every moment by every living being. HELP is not a faith. Faith, is something you believe in and something that may change from one person to another and one epoch to the next. The Way of HELP is eternal and cannot be changed or replaced. Just as liquidity cannot be taken from water, similarly, HELP cannot be taken from living entities.

Try to live without using HELP for one day, one hour or one moment.

The Way of HELP is universal and works for *all*. The more you help yourself, the more healthy, whole and holy you become. The Way of HELP relies on The Pan Pathways to work, just as the body relies on its limbs. The word *Path* means, 'a way to journey upon'. From our Being we use Knowing, Relating and Creating to journey to and from the heart of creation, The Infinite Being, God. Once you begin to understand and use The Pan Pathways, you will *become one* with The Infinite Being instantly, and draw from the abundance of all spheres in creation. Whatever you want will come to you for what you need is already on your pathway.

The HELP Process in Practice

Helping ourselves is a natural part of our lives, as natural as breathing, playing, crying and laughing. From the day we are born to the day we die is one continuous journey of learning to help ourselves. For millions of years, help has been such a natural process of our evolution that we have not questioned how it works. How does The HELP Process actually work? To say, 'by helping each other', is not the answer. We want to understand and use the process of HELP consciously and actively.

To **help** is to **do for**, assist, support, co-operate, ease, unburden, unshackle, free, favour, rescue, comfort, heal, nurture, serve, deliver.... The word **process** means '*a way of doing*', 'a course of action', or a 'method of operation'. Everything we do for ourselves is governed by The HELP Process and by learning this process we can help ourselves in everything we do.

The HELP Process is the way of doing everything that helps. Think how much peace, ease and prosperity there would be if we could help ourselves. Be honest, is there a situation or condition where you need help? If you need help, raise your right hand – raise your right hand and say, *"God help me"*. If help is so simple, why do we need to learn The HELP Process? Well, do you know why so many are suffering in your country even though your president's oath of office ends with the right hand raised and the words 'so help me God'?

The more you are **called** to do for others, the more you will need to master The HELP Process. Why? Because HELP flows from the heart of God, and The Way of HELP will bring you all the help you need to do God's work. In order to become masters of The Way of HELP we have to know how The HELP Process works in practice.

How does The HELP Process work?

HELP works on the physical plane.

On the physical level, we help ourselves by using the limbs of our body. From the moment of birth, each one of us has used our body to help ourselves via countless actions. Look at the range of actions we human beings can perform to help ourselves, with our arms, legs, feet and hands. Since we have evolved into this body, we have gradually learned to master the limbs and the senses of our body. We have been able to help ourselves in the most extreme conditions: from making fire to keep our bodies warm in ancient times, to making space craft.

The human body is miraculous, as it can perform actions which no other earthly creature can, but why is this? On the physical level, the unique combination of our four limbs working in harmony is the most dynamic formula for action, but this is true of other creatures. What gives a human being this supernatural ability is the *meta*physical connection to The Infinite Being, God. Most earthly creatures can perform extraordinary acts of help, but the human being can help in miraculous ways. Why? Because we can use our metaphysical ability to 'tap' into the power of God. Without the power of God, humans would not have developed the *supernatural* potential to help.

HELP works on the spiritual plane.

The word spiritual means non-physical, astral, supernatural, religious, as acted on by God or proceeding from The Infinite Being. Although our species has done so much on the physical plane, our spiritual capacity to help ourselves is still in its infancy. That is why humans are struggling and suffering.

Every spiritual tradition offers God's way to help humanity. We know that with God's help everything is possible, so why are so many suffering? *"Reveal to me the way. The way to have all the help I need from God."* Imagine what we can do for ourselves with the help of God? What is stopping the flow of God's help from reaching even the most spiritual people is not the lack of belief or faith, but the way to receive God's help *continuously*.

All through the bible we are told that an invincible, invisible power is at man's command to supply every need. *"What so ever thou wilt ask, God will give it thee."* This is true, but millions of people pray everyday asking God to help, but their prayers are not answered. Why? We are told, *"when ye pray, believe ye have it."* Again this is true, but are all these people unbelievers? No. If you have not received all the help and blessings of life, you have neglected to ask or have not 'asked aright'.

Many people are trying to reach their goals in life, but without God's help they struggle and suffer. Others get God's help until the link is broken and the help runs dry. Then there are the wealthy and independent who don't think they need God's help. Without God we have nothing, in God we live, move and have our being. I cannot imagine living for one moment without the help of God. *"It is not natural strength that man possesses, but by the Lord that they bear fruit"*. Are you trying to keep a home, raise children or struggling to overcome a disease or addiction? Are you yearning to fulfil a need or ambition and suffering in silence to pay your bills, taxes, and saving for old age....? **Let God help you.**

A lot of people do not know the way to let God help them, and many do not ask because they do not believe that God can help fulfil every need. The bible says, *"if thou canst believe in this God Power, all things are possible."* What is this *God power* and how does it flow to make all things possible? You may *believe*, but what is the *way* to tap the flow and the power of God? Prayer, but we must learn the way to pray that will meet our needs. Prayer is the key to channelling the *God Power* that helps to make all things possible. But let me ask you ...How do you pray?

How does prayer work?

Prayer is a link with God and the way to get God's help. Prayer is both the way to *call* and to *channel* the invisible power of God from the spiritual realm, to manifest on the physical plane. The bible says, *"before ye call I have answered"*, and yet deeply religious people who pray for hours on end struggle to make ends meet. Why? It is not the lack of faith or belief and even if it is, God gives to the faithless to make them faithful, and the unbelieving to keep them believing. You can be a saint or a sinner. God wants to bless you *equally.*

If you are suffering, the most important *spiritual skill* you need to learn is how to pray. Prayer is the way to reunite with God and be helped to manifest the miraculous. Most people find it difficult to do the possible, a few manifest the impossible and even fewer complete the supernatural, but with God's help we can manifest the miraculous. That is spiritual common sense. By knowing how to pray *you* will possess the invincible, invisible God Power and the command of the spiritual and physical planes. Yes, you! The *most important* spiritual skill God has taught me is how to pray. Prayer is an activity which is governed by a process from *beginning* to *end*. **But where does prayer begin and end?**

Prayer begins when we *ask* and ends when we *receive*. Like transmitting a signal, we send the message by asking or offering, and receive in the way of blessings. God is the giver and we are the receiver. A prayer can therefore take a few moments, months, decades or a life time to complete. For example when I was sixteen years of age, I cried out, *"help me"*, from the core of my being. Look how God continues to help me.

By knowing the process of prayer, your life will also become *fruitful*. Do you want to know how the prayer works? Well, prayer *begins* when your being *links* with The Infinite Being and the God power flows into your Being, then Knowing, Relating, Creating and *ends* in the manifestation – a miracle.

That is how HELP works on the spiritual plane. The Pan Pathways *carry* the God Power which flows from the spiritual to the physical plane. Because these pathways are flowing continuously we are helped continuously by God. These are the four pathways which link the physical and spiritual into one process. In this way every idea originates from the spiritual and manifests in the physical. The process which makes this interaction from idea-to-completion possible is governed by The Pan Pathways.

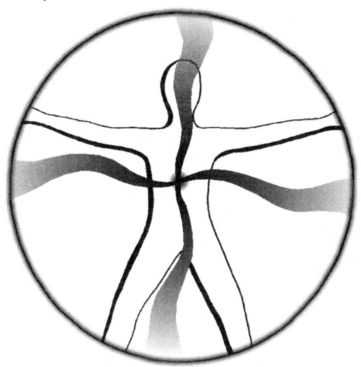

The Way of HELP is so powerful because you draw your power from both the physical and spiritual planes. A human being has the unique capacity to use the four limbs of the physical body, together with the four pathways of our spiritual body, in order to help themselves and other beings.

How does The HELP Process work in practice?

To demonstrate how The HELP Process works in practice, I have chosen a primitive act of human creation. One of the most helpful acts of human creation was the discovery of fire. The discovery of the way to make fire relieved humans from suffering cold and gave us the freedom to roam the Earth, and now to send humans into space. How did we make fire and pass on the process to each other? Well, think of how fire was made in prehistoric times. We used our limbs to collect kindle and wood, which was ignited by using flint stones to spark a fire. This same process was repeated time and time again, which is how the making of fire was passed on to following generations. Unknown to our ancient ancestors, the physical process of making a fire was governed by the very pathways which govern all human interaction.

This is how stone age man made fire: from their *Being* they had the *idea of fire*, which was coupled with their *Knowing* about kindling, wood and flint stones. By *Relating* to these elements with skills of *Creating*, they made a fire. This is how The HELP Process is practised in all other actions. The advantage of knowing how The HELP Process works is that we can create what we need and want *with mastery*. So, how do we begin to master The HELP Process? Where do we start?

We begin to practise The HELP Process by helping ourselves to build the foundations. Why is that so important? The foundations of Health, Home, Family and Work are the roots of our existence. Every act we perform is rooted in these foundations, which provide the stability and source of power to perform actions. If we are to help others, we have to be able to help ourselves, and that means nurturing our own foundations.

The most important message of HELP is to make helping oneself an *ongoing* process in daily life. Only then will HELP become your way of life and do for you what it promises. Read the following and keep coming back to this process as a reference.

How do we use The HELP Process in our daily life?

Firstly: Pray. Ask God to guide and help you – continuously. As the voice of God speaks to you, allow the message to flow into your being. Do not reason out the voice of God. Keep the condition of your being pure by separating illusion from reality*.

Secondly: Believe and do what God is telling you. If you want God to help you then *do* and *live* the way God asks you. Do you *be-live* according to the voice of God in your Being, Knowing, Relating and Creating? If so, the God Power is flowing into your life and will bless you beyond your imagination.

Thirdly: Begin to practise The HELP Process with what you need now. Pray and listen to your *natural* needs coming from your Health, Home, Family and Work. These are the roots of your life and to live *fruitfully* your foundations must be deeply rooted in God. Let God guide your Being, Knowing, Relating and Creating to manifest what you need. Choose something simple and see how The HELP Process works. Practise patiently and expectantly. In this way, slowly, steadily and surely The HELP Process will change your life.

The HELP Process will help every human being, in every situation and in every moment of the day. If after having learnt The Way of HELP it does not work for you, that is because you have not been taught correctly, or what you want is not in alignment with God. When this happens, examine the motivation behind your choices. As soon as you start practising The HELP Process, your choices will start to change in alignment with your being. Your life and environment will change for the better, since that will be your guide.

In our Being, there is a spiritual prototype of our ideal condition and your perfect state of existence. Most people are not aware of their perfect condition because they do not be-live according to God. Although they have flashes of what that may be, because of

* Illusion and reality will be explained later on.

ignorance they fail to connect with its source, and instead have contrary pictures of fear, greed, destruction and death stamped in their subconscious.

Many people try to change their circumstances by controlling other people and external events. The only person who needs to change is *you*. As you make the correct choices, all conditions of your life will change for the better, for example, did you choose your clothes today? Are you at ease? Did you choose where you live and work? Are you at peace? What is true of a little choice is true of a big choice.

> ***Look back at your life and see how you have attracted
> either happiness or disaster by your choices.***

Every choice you make, either helps or harms your Health, Home, Family and Work. A choice is like throwing a pebble in a still pond. The choices you make are very important, as what you choose sends ripples around your community. At this moment, billions of choices are being made and communicated via words, actions, images, the internet, radio and T.V., yet the *condition* of humanity and the Earth is *poor.* But what has the crisis in humanity and the poor condition of the Earth have to do with you?

You see, just as each one of us chooses to create our personal condition, our choices affect our family, community, country and humanity as a whole. The condition of the Earth and humanity is the result of choices made by individuals like you and me. Think about the choices you made at work and how they affect the condition of your co-workers, their families, friends and so on. There is a simple equation that we must teach in our schools and that each one of us needs to understand.

CHOICE = CONDITION

Practising The HELP Process

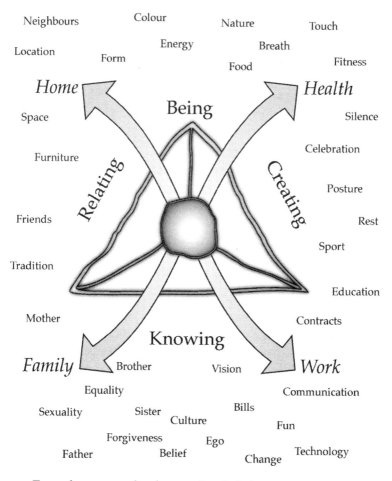

Everyday you make thousands of choices which affect your Health, Home, Family and Work. The condition of these foundations determines the condition of your Being and in turn the choices you make. If you are not living in a condition of peace and ease, the chances are you are not making the correct choices.

What happens to us, our species and the ecology is not by chance. If you can create suffering and destruction, you can choose to manifest peace and ease – Paradise. *You have the power of choice.* The HELP Process shows us how we can relieve the suffering on the Earth simply by making *helpful* choices in our own lives. By making helpful choices in your own life, you will effortlessly improve the condition of your life and the condition of the Earth, in profound ways. The HELP Process when practised, activates the life-force which flows from person-to-person, changing, creating and manifesting peace and ease in unseen ways.

Once you know how to practise The HELP Process in daily life, you can then apply it to creating whatever you wish. I believe that a human being is a supernatural being, capable of manifesting the miraculous. There is no limit to what our species can create with The HELP Process. Little did our ancestors know that the process which enabled them to make fire is the same one we now use to send humans to other planets. What kind of a world could we create if we start teaching The HELP Process in our schools, colleges, churches and work places?

The HELP Process is not a philosophy, prophecy or fad that comes and goes. It is a practical, workable process that promotes human evolution and life procreation. HELP touches all aspects of our lives. The HELP Process can be used in all facets of society: by individuals in education, services, business and organisations. The way to spread The HELP Process is to practise it yourself in order to develop your Health, Home, Family and Work. By focusing on The Foundations of HELP via The Pan Pathways, HELP will become a way of life. Peace and ease is the goal.

In order to help you get a deeper understanding of The Way of HELP we shall explore the pathways of Being, Knowing, Relating and Creating in the following chapters. There we shall discover a living Paradise on Earth.

The
Pathway
of

Being

Reflections on Being

I am free from the business whirlpool.

I have an enormous bank account of good actions, so much that I have more than enough.

I am living in accordance with my divine being.

I have awakened and can show others how to do so.

In the midst of chaos and confusion I am centred.

I know how to separate illusion from reality on the spur of the moment.

I am motivated by the awareness that all-is-one.

I am aware that the current world culture is based on illusion.

I am aware that complexity is bondage and that simplicity is freedom.

I live a simple life – look!

I can transform my pain and pleasure into Paradise.

I am guided by my intuition.

I am always in the right place at the right time.

I am completely harmless, for I am free of fear and guilt.

I do not need faith from the scriptures or sermons, because I have natural faith.

As I stand naked in the woods or at home, I feel completely safe and supported by other people and the Earth.

I devote the rest of my life to serving humanity and the Earth.

I can create miracles without possessions, power or position.

The greatest gift I have given to my family and friends is the example of my own life working.

I constantly live in a state of peace and ease, in Being itself.

The Role of Being

For thousands of years the human race has been searching for the purpose and meaning of life. In order to give us purpose, every avenue has been explored by science, religion and now through space exploration. So fruitless has been the search that most people have given up and do not take these two questions seriously:

> *What is the purpose of life?*
> *What is the meaning of life?*

You may scoff at these questions. Understandably so. Sadly, despite all our scientific and spiritual wisdom or perhaps because of the lack of it, we do not know the purpose and meaning of our lives. When we pose these questions to our parents, teachers, preachers and public figures, we get so many different answers that we must either believe there are truly many answers, or that they really do not know. Are these questions life's riddles for us to solve ourselves or is there a universal purpose for life we can embrace as our own? Have you ever pondered on the following question, even for a moment?

> *What is the purpose of my life?*

Do you know the answer, or know anyone that does? If we do not know the purpose of our lives, where are we heading and what are we living for? From what I can see, most people are without a purpose and are living for 'a lost cause'. Unless we fulfil the real purpose of our lives, *all* our efforts will be in vain. Of course many people have found and fulfilled their *vocation* in life, but this is not the *purpose of our life*. I believe that each human being has a purpose *in* life that is one and the same as the purpose *of* life. In fulfilling our *personal* purpose, we come to know the *universal* purpose and meaning of life. I know that there is *one ultimate* purpose for all human beings and in fulfilling that purpose we give meaning to our lives and become one with all other living beings. Before I reveal the purpose and meaning of life, I request that your mind be open.

The word *Being* means *essence, nature, soul, heart, core* or *centre*. Just as the heart is at the core of our body, Being is at the centre of our whole existence. Are you with me so far? By being in touch with our centre we know the nature of being human. All the searching and striving to *do* and *be* are a quest for one's own being. Without Being, humans are lost. Lost humans are always looking, praying and yearning to be with their being.

> ***Being is the purpose of life.***
> ***Being is the meaning of life.***

As simple as it is, in Being we fulfil the purpose of life and give meaning to our lives. To demonstrate what I am saying choose any purpose, aim or ideal you may have and trace it back to its origin or end. Where did you end and begin? In the same way, look closely at any object or entity in the whole of creation and tell me where it came from. Just as a human being came from another human being, every other object or entity has come into being from another, and ultimately from The Infinite Being.

By regaining this 'condition of *being*' we resume our cardinal connection with The Infinite Being. A human being who has regained this cardinal connection is the ultimate force of creation, a 'supreme human being' demonstrating a Divine way of being in the world. The role of Being is to provide human beings with a purpose and direction, i.e. to live in a condition of being and to gain the cardinal status of *being* human on this Earth.

The Earth is crawling with billions upon billions of life forms, of which humanity is one species and you are one human being. Every time you think, blink, and breathe you naturally affirm your divine right to *be*. At this moment an infinite number of creatures are breathing in and out. This makes the Earth a living being suspended in space. If we were extra-terrestrial beings observing the Earth from space, what would we see? A beautiful planet. What makes the Earth so appealing is the aggregate activities and contribution made by each grain of sand, drop of water, leaf, insect, bird, animal and *you*. So the next time you stand in awe of the Earth's beauty, remember your part in the scheme of things, for without you, this Earth would not be so appealing. Your presence and participation are vital to its continuation.

Thank you for Being here.

When we view the Earth as an extension of *our* being, we are all players, playing our part, living out our true purpose. As in any team game, no one individual or creature is more important than another. Without a single member the team would not be complete. This makes our participation and contribution *vital* to the well-being of the Earth and all its inhabitants. You are the most important person in the world, as *your way of being* in the world can destroy or promote the well-being of other creatures and the Earth. For example, you can plant one seed from which will grow millions of trees, or you can set a forest alight, leaving scars on the Earth that can be seen from space.

Why are intelligent human beings behaving in such a senseless and suicidal way? Is it because humans lack a sense of *Being,* that our minds are misguided and the Earth is being killed by our actions? Without Being to give us purpose, direction and meaning, humans are disoriented, somewhat like a raging elephant leaving behind a trail of destruction. The only way to save our species and the Earth from destruction is for each human being to live according to their Being.

Being

The Way of Being

We begin with *The Pathway of Being* because it flows from the heart of the human being. The condition of our Being is central to our *wellbeing*. It determines our direction in life and the way we live, and the way we live, in turn reflects our wellbeing. The phrase *wellbeing* appears in almost every health magazine, therapy and health care promotion, yet what does it mean and how do we actually live in that condition all the time?

Our Being is like a beacon.

Just as a beacon is a source of light, our Being is the source of inner light or intuition, which is carried via The Pathway of Being. Many people have experienced a momentary sense of wellbeing, but glimpses of this inner light are brief and we soon fall back into darkness. My aim here is to present The Pathway of Being in simple and practical ways for you to reach, and remain in the condition of *well* being.

Before we explore The Pathway to Being, it is vital that we understand what has caused the lack of wellbeing in the first place. Although there are many reasons why we do not see the inner light, they usually manifest via one activity that denies us Being. The world we live in is busy, and *being busy* takes us away from The Pathway of *Being human*. We are all busy bodies! People are taught to be busy, rather than *be human.*

If we look at any creature, a cat for example it does what is *necessary* and no more. Humans try to do more and be more than they need to be. Human beings are the only creatures that lack this natural sense of wellbeing. From a very early age children are encouraged to be busy and business like. Why? To be busy implies success, greatness and happiness. The busier you are the more you are in demand and so more people look up to you. Being busy is often seen as being worthy and we are forced to be busy or at least pretend to be.

Everyone from our primary school teachers and preachers to the presidents of our nations are all busy, but *doing what*? Do we have to be so busy to live a happy and healthy life? If this is so then who has succeeded? Is it necessary to do so much or is it *'much ado about nothing'*? You may smile, but beware of working with people who have a busy lifestyle, as unless you have the ability to 'hover and land at will', you can be sucked into the 'business whirlpool'. Once in the whirlpool, we become speed freaks hooked on adrenaline and feeling excitement as we go around at the top end. Being busy initially gives us a buzz to which we become addicted. But, in due course, we become disoriented as we are sucked into the darkness at the whirlpool's vortex. Unable to see the folly, we try to find our way out of the darkness by becoming even more busy. Busi-ness destroys lives.

How many people do you know who are not busy?

Being busy, is not necessarily a physical activity, but more a sense of hurriedness that comes from deep within. Even those who look cool and calm can be mentally busy trying to control the inner chaos within. I once lived in a monastery where the monks prayed and meditated for hours on end. These monks were so busy trying to 'save their souls', that they sacrificed the basic needs of *being human*. The more busy we become for *any* cause, the more we neglect being human itself. At this point we are ready to ask the questions: if I am in the whirlpool, what can I do about it? How can I find lasting and real fulfilment whilst continuing to be effective in the world?

To find a way out of the whirlpool, we must first know what causes its force and then find ways to become free of it. First, let us look at the cause by firstly seeing world culture as a global game show. We all participate in the game through books, magazines, movies, and especially television. In the United States of America 99.5% of all homes have television sets, and have them on for an average of eight hours a day. Electronically, the whole country is 'wired together' as a single entity.

The problem however is not television, for the whirlpool was set in motion long before the advent of television. It is not the medium but the subliminal messages coming from it which propels the global game show. Its message is a particular vision of paradise. The global game show revolves around a promise of paradise. Whether from profit, production, power, position, religion, sex, violence, education, it promises you whatever you desire to fulfil your vision of paradise, if only for a fleeting moment. The problem is that this paradise peddled by the media is an illusory one. It does not actually bring fulfilment. It only fosters more want and desire, which perpetuate the game show. To escape the whirlpool, we have to see through such fogs of illusion which prevent us from seeing the inner light.

In our quest for being more and doing more, we humans have lost sight of the inner light that should guide our lives. Because we cannot see the light, we lack a true focus in life and end up uselessly running around, even as we are trying to find the light. At this point we are poised to ask the question:

Am I busy
or
am I Being?

If we are busy for *any* purpose, how can we stop, see the light and regain our condition of being without becoming busy trying to do so?! The desire for *Being* after all is a quest like any other. It can send us running around so we become busy bodies as so called *spiritual* people often are. When I was a teenager I too was *looking for myself* . In trying to find what they called 'self-realisation' I became very busy meditating, chanting and praying, all of which made me feel good for a while but had to be repeated, as is done by millions on the spiritual path. The irony was that the constant repetition of these 'spiritual techniques', made me even busier than before. I soon realised that these techniques were in fact addictive, since they were comforting, but not the way to my being.

It became clear that the way to my Being was not via *doing, trying or finding*, but by seeing through the illusions in my mind. These illusions were like a mirage in the desert that did not really exist. I realised that I had been caught in a strange duality of existence and that my quest for *Being* would end when I had rid my mind of *all* illusions, but how would I do that? My mind was filled with thousands of illusions that had been passed on by my forebears. The act of letting them go appeared daunting and could have taken decades. The way of ridding my mind of *all* illusions would be by separating illusion from reality *in every moment.* The way to do this was revealed to me in a vision which showed me the dual existence of illusion and reality.

Knowing how to separate illusion from reality was inspiring, but facing up to the consequences was very challenging. You see, letting go of illusions which we had previously believed to be real can evoke fear and resistance, since the mind is entering the realm of reality. Separating illusion from reality *in every moment of the day*, for the first few months feels like falling into an abyss. There is nothing to hold on to, no foothold to stand upon, as everything we believed real and therefore based our lives upon is revealed to be illusory! As we shall see, the process of separating illusion from reality is simple, clear and easy to use. Do not however, underestimate the effect it will have on your life. Be aware that this knowledge once activated, will lead to a shift in your consciousness at the primal level, as that is where the inner light is blocked from your Being.

People often ask me: what is Being? I am not able to tell them what Being is, for it is a state of existence which is beyond speech.

I can however explain *the way* to Being itself. The way to Being begins by acknowledging its actual existence. In our busi-ness to get to where we want to be, we have denied or become blind to the part of a human which we call *Being,* hence, human being. This aspect of our nature is out of focus or out of sight and that is why it is spoken of so rarely. The question is: how can we get in touch with a part of us that we don't even know exists, let alone live in that state?

We must start by coming to terms with the notion that generation after generation have focused on the material and mental development of our culture. Humanity as a whole has become blinded. Like a blinkered race horse it no longer has all round vision. The way to Being is in a direction which is new to the human mind, but the mind must learn a new way of seeing in order to see the inner light of Being. Although Being is at the centre of our existence, our focus in life is 'off-centre' and needs to be realigned to its 'true-centre'. The following simple experiment will, in part, demonstrate what I am trying to explain.

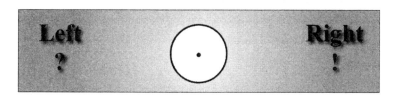

The eye's blind spot. Hold the book four to five inches (10 -12 cm) from the face. Shut one eye and fix the other on the dot. Move your head from left to right and the question mark or exclamation mark will appear and disappear.

Our Being lies behind the blind spot of our awareness. We know that such a place exists because sometimes we 'see the light' coming from it and in rare moments we can see it head on. In theory, all this makes sense, but in the history of humanity so have many speculations on the nature of being. We are still left wondering where our Being is and how we can actually see it.

How can we see through the fog of tradition and illusion that prevents us from Knowing our way to Being?

Firstly we need to acknowledge that Being is part of our daily lives and not some far-fetched experience reserved for the privileged few. Secondly, we must realise that we can live in our own Being, simply by making choices which enhance the quality and condition of our lives. Life's equation is very simple. If you make bad decisions, you suffer the consequences and with every good decision you make comes a more comfortable condition of life. Hence, how you feel now, is the result of a long line of decisions you have made in the past. Of course our decisions and daily lives are influenced by our upbringing and surroundings, but, once we know the pitfalls, we can avoid tripping up by consciously choosing the most appropriate courses of direction and action.

However, to make such wise decisions, we need the wisdom to know what is true or false, illusion or reality. Wisdom takes a lifetime to develop, or so we are told! The dilemma is: if the wisdom to separate illusion from reality takes a lifetime and special circumstances to develop, what use is it to anyone, especially the young? Life happens in the moment, and to make the most out of it, we have to make life-enhancing choices. To make such choices we must know how to see every situation for what it is and this requires the wisdom of separating illusion from reality. That may sound obvious, but if we already knew how to do this then we would not have so much suffering and destruction in the world.

In my teenage years I used to read sacred scriptures and seek guidance from enlightened people who spoke of good and evil, sins and salvation of my soul. Whilst their words were interesting and inspiring, they remained just that: words which were of little use *on the street.* I realised that true spirituality or enlightenment is demonstrated by making choices based on reality. How do you separate illusion from reality in *every thought, moment and encounter?* What we need then, is a simple method to help us separate truth from falsehood and illusion from reality, *on the spur of the moment,* since that is how life's decisions are made. The following process is so simple and effective that it can be used by *everyone* to make their perception razor sharp.

We begin by building on the notion that the world is composed of opposites, e.g. night and day, front and back, inside and outside etc. Illusion and reality are also opposites and exist simultaneously within and without. Knowing which one is illusion or reality is the key to making the choices that will lead you to live a *true life.*

The idea of living a true life sounds very spiritual, but how do we realise it when so many have tried and fallen short. We often hear phrases such as, 'living in darkness or light', 'living a lie', or 'living religiously', but what do they mean and how do we actually move from falsehood to a 'true way of life'?

How do I live a true life?

Living a true life or a false one has its origins in what we *see* and *follow.* I believe that human beings are caught in a strange duality of existence, where illusion and reality are not clearly seen and separated. The lack of clarity has led to the creation of an 'illusioned' world culture on which lives are founded. The human mind must clearly see the difference between illusion and reality. Only then can we choose reality over illusion and live a true life, but how can we see through thousands of illusions?

To help the human mind to see the difference between illusion and reality, I would like to share a vision of what I call the *Realms of Illusion and Reality.* Unless you are already living a true life, the clarity of separating illusion and reality will make you review your whole approach to your life and change your central beliefs. This is how it will work. The more you follow the Realm of Illusions the more you live a false life, but by following the Realm of Reality you will live a true life. These realms illuminate who we are and the way we live, both in private and public. What I have created reveals the realm that I saw and followed. Honesty is the key that opens the door to a true life, because the denial of the truth/reality is a judgement of an illusioned mind used to justify the living of a false life.

What you are about to see may radically change the way you live forever. What I am about to say will level the illusionary world culture to dust and the realm of reality will reign supreme.

This process will awaken people. People are asleep in the Adamic dream of opposites where lack, loss, failure, sin and sickness are seen as realities. The story of Adam is that he ate from the fruit of illusion and fell into a deep sleep. In this sleep he vaguely imagined good and evil. In doing so, he invented the opposites in his mind. He created the reasoning mind, which has come to dominate all our choices throughout the ages. Of course Adam stands for the Generic Mind.

When Adam vaguely imagined good and evil, there began a dualistic way of being, based on illusion-darkness, flesh and ignorance. The duality of good and evil, in due course gave rise to the 'creation' of Heaven and Hell. Heaven is where good people go and Hell is for the evil people. The other four illusions of gain and loss, success and failure, great and small and right and wrong perpetuate the world of good and evil.

The story of the *Garden of Eden* portrays Paradise: reality perceived by the super-consciousness where whatever we need is always at hand. With the development of the *illusionary* mind, we have reasoned ourselves into, lack, loss, limitation and failure. Over generations we have learnt how to earn our bread by the sweat of our brow, instead of *being* Divinely provided for. The time has come to free ourselves from illusions and procreate the Garden of Eden. The following five steps will intuitively guide all to reconnect with reality. *They are a reality check.*

ILLUSION*	REALITY*
GAIN & LOSS	NEUTRALITY
SUCCESS & FAILURE	CONTENTMENT
GREAT & SMALL	I AM THAT I AM
RIGHT & WRONG	DISCRETION
HEAVEN & HELL	NOW

Pan Pathways: Realms of Illusion and Reality

If you are following the Realm of Illusion, then you will be suffering from lack, worry, mistrust, jealousy, hate, anger, arrogance… By making choices based on the Realm of Reality you will experience peace, ease, plenty, love, trust, humility, joy… *You choose!*

* Reality means property of being real or original.   * Illusion means deception or delusion.

Neutrality is the first step we must take toward the discovery of reality. Everything in and around us is moving, and whenever there is a movement, there is change. Haereditas said, *"one can never step in the same river twice"*. Life is like a river and the more we flow with it, the less we suffer. We suffer because we get stuck on its banks or try to stop its flow. When we flow, we can adapt to change constantly, not by anticipation, but as it happens. We tend to think that when we let go and flow, we will lose what we gained, i.e. money, material things and land etc. Our society views life in terms of profit and loss and the way we view life forms our reality.

The current world culture is based on the idea of *gain and loss*. Although there is enough for everyone, gain, greed and desire outweigh what we actually need. Greed is born from the fear of not having enough. The irony is that what we fear most will happen to us. If you yearn for gain, then loss becomes the enemy within. The fear of loss drives people to compete against each other. Individuals who are competitive are motivated by fear, be they winners or losers. Fear breeds fear and makes us fixed, holding on to beliefs and ideas. We soon close down and cocoon ourselves.

Life around us however, is always changing. Everything we need and all we could want surrounds us, but in a separated state we can neither receive or give. This is why billions of people are living in a repetitive cycle of suffering.

You see in every passing moment, billions of people make decisions that are based on gain and loss. Their decisions result in fierce *competition – a deadly virus* that is destroying humanity and the Earth. Ironically the cure for this disease costs nothing, since we are born with it – neutrality. Neutrality, is the ability to view change as a neutral event. To be free of the illusion of gain and loss, one has to become neutral towards the events of the world. This neutrality is expressed in the form of a 'Divine judge', witnessing the drama of gain and loss. Some people may be winning the lottery or losing a fortune, inheriting land and property, cheating in business, being sent to prison or being put in a position of power. In the seesaw of society, the 'judge' must remain neutral, flowing and changing, and have nothing to do with gain and loss.

Contentment is the second step towards living in realisation. It is the natural state of every living thing. Having done its daily chores, it returns to a state of rest and relaxation. Beauty is a relaxed human being who is content. That is why babies are so appealing. Adults however, after having all they need and want are still not content and yearn for more, in the belief that there is never enough. This yearning for more is propelled by the subconscious fear that life does not support us and to survive we must have more and more.

The whole world culture is consequently based on the illusion of *success and failure* which feeds itself on the hierarchy of winners and losers, of which *you* are one. Society idolises winners, and 'success is the place to be'. Losers, are failures to be rejected on the scrap heap of 'disposable people'. Ironically, sooner or later everyone fails, since *success is simply the postponement of failure*. Think about it! If success is such a great place to be, in looking at the successful people of history and today, we must ask ourselves: do we want to end up like them? Success fears failure and the fear of failure drives people to succeed.

Success and failure are like a mirage.

People spend their entire lives climbing the ladder of success, only to find that their ladder is leaning on an illusion. Unlike the mirage of success and failure, contentment is always present, regardless of the circumstances. The aim is to realise that every time we make a decision motivated by success or failure we sow the seeds of suffering. When we see ourselves suffering, all we need to do is stop competing and be content with what we have and who we are. Even in the most dire situations we can find something to be grateful about. In being content we unleash the power and beauty of being human.

Be still for a moment and ask yourself what is missing from your life and how you can get it. The secret of contentment is in your state of mind, not your actions, possessions or the imagined future. The moment you stop yearning, you will feel content.

I am that I am, is the third realisation towards awakening because, the moment we acknowledge that we are all the same under our skin, we become equal. Yes, we are all born equal. At birth we have this awareness.

When we were infants, we just knew that we could achieve anything. We had no thought of becoming great or being good enough. This natural self-confidence or self-worth was then washed away by the continuous pounding of the status driven culture we live in. This is why most ordinary individuals believe they are too small and sheep-like to make a significant contribution to humanity. The analogy of the sheep and the shepherd has been abused by our leaders in order to protect their own position and prosperity and maintain control over the masses. We need to realise that *great and small* are relative since who is Napoleon without his army, the Pope without his cardinals or the President without his political allies?

If the founders of your faith were living today, how would they live and work? How would they dress and what would they possess? Now compare your answer with how people have been conned by the illusion of great and small to idolise position and possessions dramatised in spiritual and political rituals.

When we look at the *true* leaders in the history of humanity, we can see that they did not need to demonstrate their greatness by elevating themselves above the ordinary people or by surrounding themselves with opulence, pomp and grandeur.

In order for us to be free of the tyranny of great and small, we must beware of bowing to images and individuals simply because everyone else does. The next time you feel daunted by life or larger than life people, remember that you are no less or more than they are… I am that I am.

Discretion is the fourth step on the journey of self-realisation. Life is not made of chances – but choices, and sooner or later we need to make difficult decisions that can have lasting consequences on the rest of our lives. As we make decisions, we need to use our own discretion, based not on what is *right and wrong* in the eyes of our culture, but on what is good for *us*. Making decisions based on our own discretion will set us free from the bondage of tradition and blaze a trail into the unknown. In other words, if we use discretion to make our life decisions, we become masters of our own destiny. We will come to realise that rules, made by authorities defining right and wrong, were made without consulting us and are not necessarily valid for us in today's society or as individuals.

The majority of humanity's discoveries have been brought about by individuals who did not compare themselves with others, or care about the *right or wrong way of doing things*. For instance, Galileo as a result of observations made through his telescope, proclaimed that the Earth was not the centre of the universe. At the time this was blasphemous, and he spent many years of his life in hiding. History has shown that what was once believed to be wrong has often turned out to be the best way! Of course there are those amongst us who will proclaim that doing 'right' and being 'righteous' are the best ways to live. This may be true but if we are already living righteously, what is causing the suffering, still in our lives?

The truth is that rising above what is believed to be right and wrong, does not mean that we can act irresponsibly, just as doing what is thought to be right, does not guarantee that we are being responsible. Ask yourself, is it right or wrong to eat meat and drink alcohol? Questioning what we believe to be right or wrong can be very unnerving as it leaves us with what *is… now*. We can then, no longer rely on other people's beliefs, but must develop our own ideas and discretion in order to make decisions.

Now take the fifth and final step to *realisation*. The moment is *now*. In this moment, you have the opportunity to escape or enter the divinity of your being. If you are not ready to enter the divinity of your being now, then there will be tomorrow, next week or next year. Each time your thoughts dwell on the opportunity for realisation, it will be now. A thousand years hence, it will be the eternal now.

How can you avoid wasting this precious moment and use every moment to live in your Being? Simple, by having taken the first four steps, you will be very close to the state of *Being*. Finally then, let go of the illusion of *Heaven and Hell*, for there is no such place. The human mind has imagined Heaven and Hell as vaguely as Adam imagined good and evil.

The place called Heaven is supposed to be the dwelling place or the abode of God. Where is that and how do you get there? All the major religions have their own unique saviour and their uncompromising set of do's and don'ts, as the means to enter Heaven. The question is: if each religion has the *sole* rights to enter Heaven, then which one is *real*? Or are there many Heavens and, if so, as many Hells? Are you ready…?

Heaven is not a place, it is a state of Being with God. Now.

Let me explain. God is omnipresent, which means everywhere and in everything, here and there, in the past, present and future. God is here with me now. I can feel the love, power, wisdom and the grace of God now. Now is the most powerful moment in creation. Why? Now is always the moment for my Being to be with God… The Infinite Being. That is why I say that now is the ultimate reality and God is the absolute realisation.

Be aware that you are here – now. God is within and all around you. The chase for Heaven has caused humans to step away from

Being with God. We have become lost in trying to get from here to Heaven. If you are *trying* to get from here to Heaven now, you are missing the moment of Being with God… now! If you keep missing the moment of Being with God now – and until you die, you will attain the same state in the 'next life'! God created the whole of creation and that makes the Earth a Heavenly place to be. To 'build the kingdom of Heaven on Earth', each human being has to purify their condition of Being by separating illusion from reality and live in a non-dualistic state with God. Look, my life is Heavenly: a living Paradise on Earth. Now.

The Oxford dictionary describes Heaven as the 'presence of God'. For me, Heaven is the *abode* of God and God lives in the heart of my Being. In Hebrew, the term for God, Jehova Shamma, means 'the God who is there'. God is there with you, but are you with God? Heaven is a place where there is no resistance to God, when we are united with God.

The realm of illusion and reality will purify your mind and body. With your mind and body purified, you will be free from illusion and the duality of existence. Being is a condition of non-dual existence. A perfect being of perfect wisdom with The Infinite Being, God.

Pain & Pleasure

For most of us, life in the physical world began when we heard screams of pain from our mother. We were given a slap on the bottom to make us cry and felt the first burning breath of dry air in our lungs. We were then subjected to bright lights, loud noises and were wrapped in towels which felt like sand paper next to our hypersensitive skin. We were introduced to life through pain and now these initial layers of memory are thought to govern our every action and reaction.

Our lives are still affected by pain, and we spend considerable time and energy trying to manage pain or painful experiences, be they of a physical, emotional or mental nature. Clearly, we need to retain the ability to feel pain, since without it we would not know when things are hurting us. The question is: how much pain do we need to feel in order to be happy, healthy human beings? Can we have too much pain and become addicted to it, just as we do with other stimulating activities such as eating, drinking, running, and meditating?

The truth is that pain leads to suffering. This may sometimes be necessary for us to learn certain lessons, and perhaps even for the salvation of humanity as a whole. But, is it possible that pain and suffering are a subtle form of torture which leaves in its wake diseased and damaged human beings? If what I am saying is true, then how does the idea and practice of universal suffering promote individual wellbeing? Why is humanity still hell-bent on destroying itself and the Earth considering all the pain and suffering experienced in human history? Is it possible that the majority of the human population is addicted to pain and that this is why we keep recreating so much suffering in diverse situations? A brief look at the news will reveal our preoccupation with spreading information on pain and violence.

If pain and suffering are harmful to our well-being, why do we create and tolerate so much? The pain I speak of is not only physical, but emotional, which lasts much longer, goes deeper and affects the whole human being. Most people know very little about pain and do not know how to deal with the symptoms of it. We tend to live in denial, because showing that one is in pain is considered a weakness and not desirable. To demonstrate my point, here are a few symptoms of pain: worry, guilt, anxiety, grief, depression, loneliness, abuse, rejection, heartache, fear, hopelessness, abandonment and ridicule. Externally we behave as though everything is well, but, be honest, how much pain do you hide?

Human beings are hooked on pain and, like junkies, live in denial of their addiction. Because we deny our pain we ignore its symptoms and try to make them go away by using other addictions. These provide only momentary pleasure, leaving us to prepare ourselves for the next bout of pain. Strangely pleasure lasts only a fleeting moment, whilst suffering lasts much longer!

Pain is the main addictive drug of humanity which is freely available to all ages and races around the world. Being addicted to pain and suffering is the ultimate addiction as *all* other addictions merely serve as the *opium* of the people and make our deranged existence tolerable.

Humanity's addiction to pain may be difficult to accept, but why are human beings subjecting themselves, other living things and the Earth to so much suffering? What would happen if all the pain that makes a human soul cry, was taken away in an instant? Over thousands of years, human beings have become so dependant on pain that our ancestors implanted potentially painful ideas and practices into religion, education, sport, art, work, entertainment and fashion in subtle and unseen ways. Today humans perpetuate and pass on this dependence to following generations. Look at the pain and painful ways of living you have inherited from your parents, teachers and society. Simple as it is, pain is a major obstacle to our well-being ...*Being*.

A Life of Simplicity

Simplicity is freedom. Simplicity comes from being free of illusion. Simplicity is an inward reality that results in an outward lifestyle. Both inward and outward aspects of simplicity are essential for well-being. We deceive ourselves if we believe we can possess the inward reality without it having a profound effect on how we live. To attempt to arrange an outward lifestyle of simplicity without the inward reality, leads to deadly confusion and panic. Inward reality begins with inward simplicity and unity. It means living from the centre of our Being.

Experiencing inward simplicity liberates us outwardly – speech becomes truthful and honest. The lust for status and position is gone, because we do not need status and position to live in the *divine centre*. Without the divine centre, our need for security leads us into an insane attachment to 'things'. Inwardly, we are fractured and fragmented, and trapped in the maze of competing attachments. One moment we make decisions on the basis of realisation and the next moment out of fear, i.e. the illusion of what others will think of us. Humanity has no unity or focus concerning the orientation of life. Contemporary culture lacks both the inward realisation and the outward lifestyle of simplicity.

We must clearly understand that the lust for affluence is psychotic because it has completely lost touch with reality. We crave for things we neither need nor enjoy. We are made to feel ashamed to wear the same clothes or to use objects until they are worn out. The mass media has convinced us that to be out of step with fashion is to be out of step with reality. It is time we awaken to the fact that to be healthy in a sick society means that sick people think *you* are sick!

Although I cannot describe all the inner ways of experiencing simplicity, I would like to mention ten ideas for the outward expression of simplicity. They should not be viewed as laws but as one attempt to flush out the misunderstanding of simplicity in twenty-first century life.

- ~ Buy things for their usefulness rather than their status.
- ~ Reject anything that is producing an addiction in you.
- ~ Develop the habit of giving things away.
- ~ Throw away or sell everything you do not need.
- ~ Learn to enjoy things without owning them.
- ~ Develop a deeper appreciation for creation. Get close to the Earth.
- ~ Avoid buying too much food, drink, clothes etc.
- ~ Use plain and honest speech.
- ~ Reject anything that will breed oppression in others.
- ~ Shun whatever would distract you from your main goal.

A life of simplicity does not mean that you live in poverty and austerity. No, simplicity goes hand in hand with prosperity. When your life is simple, your *faith* and *focus* in life is directed towards what you *really* need, want and wish. Look, my life is a living example of how simplicity and prosperity go hand in hand.

Fear and Faith

Over ninety-five per cent of our behaviour is a repetition of yesterday. This is fine if you are happy, but if you are suffering, what then? What is it that makes us repeat the same patterns of behaviour day after day, decade after decade, and generation after generation? There are many reasons, but they all stem from one source – FEAR. Fear of what? Fear of *change*. Why change? Well, change by its very nature means going into the unknown. We fear the future because we do not know what will happen to us. Change is going to occur between now and then. We cannot control what has not happened yet and that uncertainty leads to hesitancy, anxiety, and fear.

> **Fear is not a reality,**
> **it is a state of mind.**

The understanding of fear and faith is relevant to becoming a whole human being. We have seen that change evokes fear within us. We cannot escape change, because change is forever present in the universe. However, *Being* is the only part of our nature that does not change. In this state of Being there is no fear because there is no change, but how do we get to this state of Being? It is very simple, by having FAITH. As we have already seen, it is doubt which leads to fear and faithlessness.

Almost everything we do, say and think is motivated either by fear or faith. Every day we have thousands of doubts and fears. Even the thought of holding someone's hand evokes fear in us. The world we live in is rife with such fear, e.g. success and failure, profit and loss, life and death, etc. So how do we move from a life of fear, to one based on faith, especially when most people are motivated by fear? Faith comes from our Being, because our Being is the pathway to The Infinite Being and unlimited faith.

Try this simple exercise. Close your eyes and hold your arms wide apart while pointing your index fingers outward. The aim is to bring the tips of the index fingers to touch at one point. Whether you made contact or missed is not the issue. The question is: was there the slightest of doubt? That doubt contains fear.

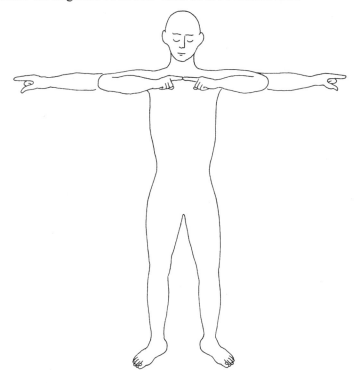

No one can give you faith. You cannot get it from reading the scriptures or sermons. Faith can only be demonstrated. What use would the scriptures and the sermons of your preachers be if it were not for the founders of your faith, who *demonstrated* the faith of the living God. There is no such thing as blind faith. Faith is anything but blind. To gain faith one must be ready to see it, not with our intellect, or eyes, but with our insight which is *seeing with our mind's eye.*

The fear that exists within and outside us, has made us blind to the faith we once had. For example, a new born creature, be it animal or human, has little or no fear of anything or anyone. It naturally believes that the world is a safe place to *be* in. That *Being* is the same in every living thing. Faith is therefore inherent to a human being. The baby does not have fear, because it is still living in that state of being called natural faith. Since it has no fear, it does not need faith to overcome it.

The way to regain the condition of natural faith is by simply believing in your own being, not in anything or anyone, but *in yourself*. Here is a demonstration of the power of faith placed within your being.

Before you were conceived, you completed a journey equivalent to swimming a thousand miles. You did the seemingly impossible. Compare what you want to do today with that achievement. Take notice of how you feel and think. You are here.... now. Make an affirmation: *"I believe in me."*

Real faith is demonstrated in what we believe and the way we live. To believe means to be-live. Many people believe in God, but do not be-live the way of God. To live what you believe demands *total* faith. There is no in-between – it is fear or faith.

Believing in yourself is the step that will lead you from fear to faith. By having faith in yourself, you will have faith in your work, vision, and future. Fearless faith will result in you having no resistance to change. When we stop resisting change, we live *in the moment* without fear. That is when a truly daring adventure will begin.

Being in Practice

At one time I was a soldier in a war. My life was very near death. I felt totally lost in the chaos and carnage around me. Life and death had become insignificant and no one had any control over what was happening or who was going to live or die. I could not work out who I was, where I was, what was happening and why I was alive. Nothing seemed to matter in those timeless moments, as if life and death meant nothing and were not important in the first place. In the middle of all this, there was a part of me that remained unaffected by the whole aimless sequence of events. Somehow I stayed perfectly still and this part of me whispered, "*Being... Being itself*". In those moments I realised that *Being*, was the purpose of my life.

My aim is to show you how to live in this condition of Being and harness its power, so that you may practise *your* way of being in the world. Many people believe that being is something spiritually sublime and beyond the reach of ordinary mortals but the truth is, it is simple and *rooted in daily life*.

Within our Being there is limitless power to help ourselves and influence the course of events all around us, and yet, why do so many people struggle to make ends meet at a most basic level? When we look at the lives of Krishna, Buddha, Jesus, and Mohammed, we are amazed at their power to help change the course of history. You have the same power. How can you tap into that power and where does it come from?

All power is in your Being.

I will show you how you can harness your power via The Pathway of Being. You are a human being, created by the Creator... The Infinite Being. In your body *lives* a very powerful Being and this Being is the same in every living being. The Pathway of Being connects you to your being and that is why you have access to the power of The Infinite Being. So if you feel powerless, it is because The Pathway of Being which channels your power is blocked and by opening this pathway you regain your power.

The way to enter The Pathway of Being is by seeing and following the realm of reality, which is like a beacon that guides you. In knowing that you are guided and powered by your being, you will start relating to the world accordingly. Once you enter The Pathway of Being, the other pathways of Knowing, Relating and Creating will also open. For example, sit quietly for a while and separate illusion from reality. *Feel the power of Being.* Then choose an area of your life that you would like to enhance or expand. Know that if you can imagine a *real* wish, you can create it, because you are guided by your Being. You will find yourself talking to your Being and asking for guidance and knowing intuitively what to do and where to go, what to ask for and what to say. You will relate to the outside world with your body, mind, feelings and your spirit, which are now aligned with The Infinite Being.

As you remember and practise The Pathway of Being, you will become a more powerful human being, feeling extremely powerful. You will be empowering the whole of your being, every cell, thought, feeling and action. Your whole being will vibrate and glow like a bright light originating from the centre of your being. As this happens, be aware of how 'bright the light shines' and the manner in which you will affect others. If you discover any detrimental effects on others, make whatever adjustments are necessary, so that your power and presence of Being is good for everyone.

The power I speak of is not the power of tyrants to dominate and exploit the weak, but the power which empowers the powerless. To ensure that the power we exercise is emanating from our Being, we simply realign our motives with the Realm of

Reality. There are many individuals who are in possession of a lot of power, but their power is based on illusion, and acknowledged by those who are guided by illusion. Is it any wonder that so many of our leaders are powerless and unable to help their people. A human being who is really in alignment with their Being is a supremely powerful person, capable of helping countless people and using power that changes events without position or possessions. The condition of such a being is pure and so powerful that the positive force is an influence for hundreds and thousands of miles.

The condition of your Being creates and controls events *far* and *wide*, *now* and in the *future*. Your Being is behind the scenes of the drama of your life, as far and wide as you can imagine. This is how it works. The condition of my Being, *now*, influences you at this moment. My condition of Being is behind what I am saying now and travels far and wide via the pathways of Knowing, Relating and Creating, to your Being.

In the same way, the present condition of my Being will create and control events now and in the future. Look how the founder of your faith is influencing the condition of your Being, your actions and your world. Now do you understand what I mean by the Being behind the scenes? What kind of Being is behind the scenes in your life?

> *Now*   *Open your eyes and look at me.*
> *Where?*   *I am at the centre of your Being.*
> *Come*   *Follow the pathways to your Being.*
> *Why?*   *To live with me in Eternal Paradise.*

Reflections on Knowing

I know how to live and what to seek.

I know what my real needs are.

I know that as I fulfil my own needs I become more happy and healthy.

I use every adversity as an opportunity for prosperity.

I know how to find solutions to seemingly impossible problems.

I know how to gain access to new knowledge from inside myself.

Whereas I used to get stuck with my own and other people's patterns of behaviour, now I glide effortlessly.

I am free of addictions and attachments and can show others how to become so.

I have infinite patience and know how to use it everyday.

I have plenty of time to do the things I love to and need to do.

I know what it means to be a custodian of the Earth and the keeper of the knowledge contained in the wilderness.

I know the difference between knowledge and knowing.

I know how to handle the thousands of mystical experiences which exist beyond the realm of rational explanation.

I am fully aware of the effects of the news on my own psyche and that of humanity.

I know how to dissolve resistance within and outside myself.

I am completely honest and therefore a force of nature.

I know how to wield absolute power.

I know that all of the suffering in the world is caused by the denial of my own soul.

I know what is true for me is true for all.

I am the master of my own destiny, my life is paradise.

The Role of Knowing

As the sun came over the horizon once again this morning, millions of human beings awoke to play their part in society. Something inside us stirred as we began to think, act and feel our way into the day which will soon come to an end. How will *you* spend the day, wisely or wastefully? We tend to think that we know how to live, but what kind of life have we lived? When we look at the lives of our parents, grand parents and great-grand parents, how did they live and what kind of legacy did they leave for us? Money, materials, land, property, and position are all useful, but without knowing how to live they make our lives wasteful. No matter how powerful, prosperous or wise you may be, if you do not know how to live, your life has been wasted. Ask yourself:

What is the best thing for me to seek?
What is the best way for me to live?

Knowing what to seek and how to live may sound obvious, especially to those who are 'spiritually enlightened', but how often do we see our spiritual leaders living in the realm of illusion? It is because we do not know how to live that we abuse ourselves, our family, friends and people in society, all be it *unknowingly.* If you really knew how to live, and what to seek, your life would be a living paradise. What kind of responsibility would we fulfil in society? Would we participate in hierarchies, profiteering, crime, corruption and exploitation?

Our society is a reflection of our lives, which in turn reflects what we believe and seek, and the traditions we live by. We are encouraged to seek and live our lives according to the norms and morals laid down by tradition. Almost everything we believe and seek in life is guided by traditional values. Those norms and values have been passed on from one generation to the next via, socialisation, education, and religion in order to maintain control and continuity within our society. The nature of tradition is so powerful and persuasive, that very little has changed at the *core* of our culture for over six thousand years. So deep are the ways of behaviour and societal expectations ingrained in our psyche, that we obey them instinctively.

The question is: what are our values and codes of conduct based on, illusion or reality? We are encouraged to compete with each other from a very early age. What if competing to win stems from fear and greed which are based on the illusion of gain and loss? Our whole world culture runs on competition and even spiritual people compete in their society, without knowing that their actions cause rifts between the rich and poor. We all know about the immense suffering in our society and complain bitterly, but what part are *we* playing, albeit unknowingly? We *really* do not know what is causing the suffering nor how to change it, for if we did, humanity would not be locked in a way of thinking that has repeated the same pattern of suffering for thousands of years.

How can we free ourselves from the cycle of eternal suffering?

Every prophet that has come wanted to impart knowledge to set us free from suffering. The knowledge was presented in many forms, from tablets of stone and revelations, to scrolls. The purpose of all this knowledge has been to allow us to relieve human suffering and live in harmony on the Earth. The history of world religion, however, reveals the same old pattern of hope and suffering, creation and destruction, except now we are on the verge of destroying the very planet on which the earthly paradise was to be built. Why has humanity not been able to establish that earthly paradise despite all the knowledge handed down by prophets, prophecies and sacred chronicles? Could it be that all this knowledge has not been used or understood? If this is so, how can we change the flaw in our way of thinking, and free ourselves once and for all? Every race has amassed knowledge over the ages, but something fundamental is lacking in our way of thinking, and that is why we are *trapped* in a cycle of eternal suffering, but what is this trap? The answer is not more of the same knowledge, since that has not worked. What we need now is to become aware of a completely new *source* of knowledge that is flowing through us constantly, as we seek what is best and live accordingly.

Does anyone know the way to eternal freedom?

Knowing is the way to eternal freedom. Knowing how to escape the flaw in our way of thinking will set us free from all repetitive patterns, but what is the difference between knowledge and knowing? When I was discovering The Way of HELP, ideas came from outside the sphere of existing human knowledge. HELP is a completely new and original way, without precedent or equivalent. I call this *Knowing*, since it is of our own making or our situation. Let me give you an example: to avoid falling into a trap we need to know where it is, but what about getting out of a trap we are already in? This requires Knowing and it is Knowing that humanity needs in order to escape from the cycle of eternal suffering. It needs a kind of knowing which is all encompassing and current, so that we can create and recreate in order to finally establish an earthly paradise.

The Role of Knowing is to set each human being free to dream, envision, imagine, reason and think their own thoughts. No longer will we be reliant on the guidance of prophets or scriptures, or will we be misguided by the false knowledge of tradition and illusion. As the day passes from dawn to dusk, let me ask *you* a question. Are you awake? If you *think* you are awake, then you are still asleep. You must *know* that you are awake!

The Way of Knowing

The quest for knowledge has been central to the evolution of our species. Knowledge is central to our existence because it enables us to make informed choices, solve problems, and create new possibilities. With knowledge we can survive, create, prosper and control our destiny. Knowledge is the key to freedom and, over the ages, countless people in all kinds of human activity have devoted their lives to preserving and adding to the body of human knowledge. The urge to learn has been so powerful that individuals have been known to sacrifice their lives to the quest for *new* knowledge. It is the quest for new knowledge that I call Knowing. Is there a difference between knowledge and Knowing? Yes:

> **Knowledge is fixed and finite.**
> **Knowing is flowing and infinite.**

From a very early age, we are conditioned to *absorb* information from books, lectures, computers and televisions, etc. Our minds are an enormous store house of knowledge that we use to accomplish our aims and aspirations, but have we ever found the *source* of *our* knowledge and the *way* to use it?

Humanity has amassed a vast body of knowledge which we have used to create and control our environment. Thanks to the body of human knowledge we have mastered other species and altered the landscape of the Earth. Despite all our knowledge and accomplishments however, I cannot help feeling sad about human suffering and the destruction of the Earth. The way humans have used their knowledge has made me question its source, purity and use. Is the knowledge that we possess impure or have we simply abused it? The answer is implicit in both these questions since the knowledge we have determines the way we use it. Can knowledge be pure or impure, like gold? Yes. If truth can be distorted then knowledge can be mixed with ill-founded aims and aspirations, which lead to impure knowledge. The human mind has been misguided by its 'source of knowledge'.

Suffering and destruction is the result of using knowledge to manifest misguided aims. Clearly there is a fundamental flaw in the main body of human knowledge, or our species would be living in peace and ease. What is this flaw, and even if we find it, how can we correct the whole body of human knowledge? Can we purify knowledge as we purify gold, and if so, how can impure knowledge be purified?

The answer lies in The Way of Knowing. Our aim must be, not amassing more knowledge, but using it in a pure way that is guided by The Infinite Being. *The Way of Knowing is not 'a body of knowledge' but a way of knowing.* The way to purify knowledge is by *knowing* the source of pure knowledge and then 'bathing in it'. For example, when our bodies become dirty, we bathe in clean water. If the source of the water is dirty our body will remain dirty. The Way of Knowing guides the mind to the source of pure knowledge, which manifests in pure ways of application.

Coming to terms with the fact that the knowledge we possess is impure may be unacceptable to some, especially when they have spent time, money and effort in acquiring it! This is understandable. Imagine if someone told you that your priceless gold watch was made of impure gold. Would there be disbelief? Similarly, the knowledge we have will not allow us to believe that it is impure or that we are using it in impure ways. The transition from becoming aware of completely new knowledge, to its actual understanding and *use,* is often a gradual process.

This is how The Way of Knowing will be approached. When people confront a new item of knowledge, they check it out against what they already know, but what if something comes along which cannot be compared with any previous knowledge? What can we do? We can ignore the new information, deny that it exists or wait until the new information becomes so apparent that the old knowledge can be discarded or modified into the new.

A new idea is often rejected and ridiculed, but to say that the whole body of human knowledge is impure will trigger a powerful reaction from all fields of knowledge. I find this understandable and acceptable, since it further demonstrates the insecurity surrounding knowledge in the sciences, religion, art and education, etc. My aim is not to provoke, but to provide help for those who are ready to consider a new way of knowing.

Firstly, let us consider how the knowledge we've been given by our family, schools, universities and society at large affects the way we are. What we seek and the way we live is determined by the way we think. The way we think is based on the knowledge we possess and the way we use it. The way people live, has to a large extent remained unchanged over the centuries. This is fine, if the lives people lead give them true freedom and fulfilment, but not if their knowledge is holding them prisoner to a limited way of life. Does the following pattern ring true for the way *you* live your life?

> *We're born. We live in a cot, then we're walking and talking. We go to school, and maybe college. We fall in love and get a job. We get married and buy a house. We go on holiday, and change job. We start a business, borrow more money and work long hours. We fall ill. We save for our daughter's wedding. We get divorced. Our life falls apart, we consider committing suicide. We think about retiring. We retire. We've lived, so we wait to die.*

Before we die, our life will pass before us but what will we see? With all the knowledge we possess, how have people come to live life like hamsters in a wheel? How can we change a way of existence which is so ingrained in our psyche? What will trigger the change? The obvious answer is the way we think, but the way we think stems from our knowledge! Each day, we have thousands of thoughts and a great many feelings, yet the way we think and live is in turmoil. Clearly the way we think is the way we behave, and the way to change our behaviour is by changing the way we think. But how can we change the way we think, when we get the same information and knowledge, time and time again?

Many people make an effort to think positive thoughts, but end up following the same pattern time after time, often not knowing the reason why. The answer lies in our conditioning.

The process of conditioning begins at birth. As we absorb the aims and aspirations of our families and society at large. Our minds enter a kind of tunnel where thoughts can move in only one direction. We may think we have the freedom to believe what we want and behave as we wish, but the thoughts we have originate from the same source and lead to the same outcome. Is this freedom?

Are you a free man or woman, or are you enslaved by the trappings of a culture that's based on illusions?

The freedom I speak of is not in order to invent new machines, discover new medicines, rebel against authority or become extremely rich. By **freedom** I mean a life lived without illusion, with the purity and innocence of a new born baby. Most human beings are like blind men, in a dark room, looking for a black cat that isn't even there! This may seem funny, but realise that the untold suffering in the world is due to this blindness. The question is: how can we wake up to our situation? What can we do to free ourselves from these repetitive ways of thinking?

The solution is much simpler than we may think. We begin by knowing and nurturing our real needs. Knowing begins with common sense, for example, when we are hungry we eat. In the same way, when we feel uncomfortable, we do what is necessary to feel better. A dog that sits on a thorn will get up. A hungry dog sniffs out food, but humans have been conditioned by 'knowledge', to take a less direct route. We take painkillers for the pain of life's 'thorns' as well as hunger. If we feel bad we take 'a drink' to feel better. In all this we remain blinkered to *knowing* the cause and the remedy. Happiness for all humans is simple, just as it is for cats, dogs, dolphins and you and me. So why don't we move directly to it? This is because we have received mistaken knowledge about life, about what to seek and how to live.

> *Knowledge is like a map.*
> *Knowing is the reader.*

If the map is wrong, its routes will take you nowhere. The map of illusion has misguided routes and false destinations – a mirage, and yet we hold on to this map with a desperate grip. We call it, 'a grip on reality' and believe in it, convinced of its authenticity, because we are *told* it is so. The funny thing is that we don't need a map, because what we seek is right here underneath our skin. Is it surprising that we cannot find real satisfaction in a career, a can of beer or in driving an expensive car!

Stop the futile search on this endless path, and get to *know* yourself and your real needs. The primary purpose of Knowing is to become conscious of your needs and how to fulfil them. In Knowing what you are and what you want, you will move from being a victim of your knowledge to being self-directed.

The freedom humans yearn for has been dangled like a carrot to a donkey for many generations. How many people do you know who are really free? We often hear terms such as salvation, transcendence, and enlightenment in spiritual doctrines, but where are the people who demonstrate freedom of will in *daily life*? How can we be freed by those who are not free? We have to find new ways of knowing. Where do we begin and who do we ask?

Before I explain The Way of Knowing, I need to 'prepare the ground', for you to fully understand how it works. In my own 'journey to freedom', I have used a simple process which *triggers* the human mind into a new way of thinking and solving problems. The following process can be used in every situation and applied on every level. The more you use it, the more you will become aware of its awesome potential to free you.

Are you ready? Imagine you are a fly that has flown into a bottle lying on its side. The drink in the bottle is sweet and other flies have flown in. As night falls, someone lights a candle that is close to the bottom end of the bottle. Now the bottle has become a trap, since all the flies will try to escape by flying towards the light. They will do this until they are dead and yet freedom and life are only seconds away! What would you do?

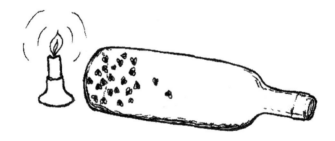

Moving the candle to the other end of the bottle may initially result in chaos, but the chances are high that most, if not all the flies, will find their way out. What did you learn from this analogy and how can you apply it to your *daily life*?

First, choose any situation or problem that you currently have in your life. Secondly, ask yourself how you got there. Thirdly, try new and original ways of solving the problem. After all, we are not flies, so why should we behave like them? When people are poor, for example, they try to relieve their poverty by working harder, because we are *conditioned* to work harder when life is difficult. Trying harder does not always help. I have lived with both the poorest and the richest people in the world. I know that both are walking down a different *mental* street. The difference between poverty and prosperity is as slight as the turn of the head.

The analogy of 'the flies in the bottle', can be applied to all areas of human concern, especially those where we need to relieve suffering and find solutions to otherwise impossible problems. The secret is to look out of the other end of the bottle and perceive life from another direction. By doing this we allow spontaneity and magic into our lives and we stop banging our heads against the walls of our preconditioning. Having prepared ourselves to perceive and approach situations in a new way, I shall now demonstrate how Knowing happens.

How does Knowing happen?

When I ask people this question, they are usually thrown and cannot relate to the question. What *is* the source of our knowledge? Is it the newspaper, books, magazines, radio, television or the internet? We are bombarded daily by messages we absorb in the form of information. *Knowing,* however, is not the same as having information or knowledge. It is *knowing* what is happening within and outside you. You may be asking, where does that knowing come from? The Way of Knowing reveals four sources that lead to knowing. These are: *Being Told, Reasoning, Imagining,* and *Direct Knowing* as shown in the diagram on the following page. Now I shall explain how knowing actually happens. So let us start with *being told*.

Being told how to live as well as what to seek is the most traditional and common way of knowing. Almost everything we do has been shown to us by our parents, peers, teachers and society at large. All of us learnt how to cook, clean, eat, read, write and speak by being shown via the five senses of, seeing, touching, hearing,

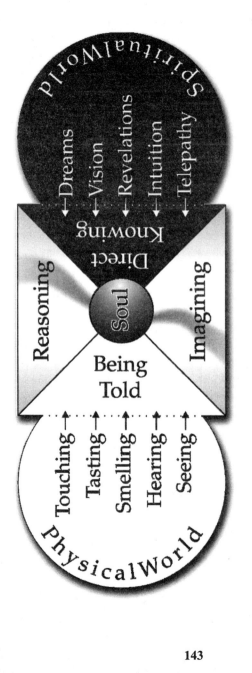

Pan Pathways: The Ways of Knowing

The Way of Knowing will open the mind and increase your metaphysical capacity to the fullest potential. Gaining mastery of all four ways of Knowing, your knowledge will be purified by all four sources. The Way of Knowing will promote the proper use of knowledge.

smelling and tasting. Being shown is the most practised form of knowing, because we can actually see and touch the external world. Its disadvantage however, lies in the possibility of absorbing impure knowledge and ill founded aspirations which we *believe* are true. Ask yourself:

How much of what I have been told is true?

The new born baby's mind is like a blank page and what we put on this page from the outset, is often central to its way of thinking for the rest of its life. A human being is a very open and vulnerable creature especially in its infancy. It can be influenced in very deep and profound ways. Children believe that what their parents tell them is *the truth* and the best way of doing things.

Being told occurs not only by instruction, but also in many subtle and unseen ways. When I was in the U.S.A., I saw many African-American men and woman who stood with their shoulders hunched and their chest slightly caved in. This position signifies the submission between the Negro slave and the white master. In fact, the slave was 'legally' freed in 1865, but the attitude of submission has been passed on subconsciously from generation to generation and few escape it. It is influencing the body and mind of men and women worldwide, even today.

In the same way, we have absorbed subtle ways of thinking and being, which our mind believes is real. Our minds are like huge flexible nets, which are designed to catch what we need but can get clogged and rigid from the debris of society. Can you bring to mind certain ways of thinking and acting that you have mirrored directly from your parents? Do they serve you, or are you suffering without even knowing why? Take a moment to ponder on this. Having been told what to do and how to do it, we must apply *reasoning* to the aim, method and motivation of the given instruction, before carrying it out, regardless of who it came from, be they parents, teachers, trainers, commanders, priests or politicians. The process of reasoning is part of the growing up process and it enables each one of us to become self-motivated and self-responsible human beings.

Reasoning is the process of making links by asking questions and experiencing life. The links are logical, i.e. "if I touch fire, it will burn me". These, 'if... then', links form chains of thought or what we call *in-form-ation*, and can be very useful, or else limit us within 'mechanical existence'.

Reasoning is a process of working things out based on what we have experienced and remembered. It includes asking questions and finding answers in order to solve problems or avoid danger, so that we can live more comfortably. The current human world culture relies heavily on knowledge that we have gained via reasoning. Our whole educational system is based on the process of reasoning: why and how things work, as well as asking in what ways we can exploit them.

Almost every choice and action, involves the reasoning of action-reaction and cause and effect. Reasoning has played a key role in the development of our mastery of the physical and material world, and now reason is the driving force behind space exploration. The laws of gravity, physics and light were discovered through reasoning. Reasoning has helped humans to survive, thrive, and exploit. Now reason is telling us that we must halt our exploitation of the Earth if our species is to continue. Pure reason is very enlightening and in due course will reveal the nature of creation via logic and mathematics.

There are however, limitations to the scope of reasoning, for it is confined to the space of existing knowledge and available information. Reasoning alone cannot show us how to paint a unique painting, create an original movement in dance, or compose a moving piece of music. To do these things we need to project our minds above and beyond our current store of knowledge.

Any good artist, scientist or social pioneer will tell you that the secret to solving impossible problems is to ask unreasonable questions. The great inventors, creators and pioneers have the capacity to combine reasoning and imagining to work their way forward into the unknown. In the same way, if we are to overcome our current crisis in evolution, we need to reason and discover what we need to change, and then *imagine* what kind of world we want to create. The reason, after all, you are reading this book is to improve the condition of your existence, coupled with your image of what your future could be.

Imagining is the process of seeing with the mind's eye. Imagining enables us to escape the two dimensional world of cause and effect and enter a surreal world without physical laws. Imagining sets us free from the limits and laws of society, as well as our current situation. Children often fantasise, daydream and imagine themselves to be train drivers, mothers, and astronauts, but as they grow we encourage them to, "get real", and "be realistic". Can you imagine the president of your nation being caught in the act of day dreaming on the beach! People would laugh and ridicule such a person, calling them immature, incompetent and incapable of leading the nation. Well Martin Luther King did just that, when he stood in front of the Washington Monument before thousands of American people and said, *"I have a dream."* The reason people believed in him was because they too could *imagine* a world *"where people are judged not by the colour of their skin but by the content of their character"*.

The freedom of imagining is that you can imagine the impossible and, in doing so, *trigger* a very powerful force that attracts whatever is necessary in order to make your vision come true. Can you imagine the sun coming over the horizon tomorrow? Well, just as you can imagine a new dawn which will happen, you can similarly imagine your future. I know this to be true, as in my youth, I wanted to live in peace and ease. Of course not knowing what it felt like to live in that condition, I had to imagine that state of existence. Today, I live in total peace and ease. Now I imagine helping humanity to live in peace and ease, a Paradise on Earth.

People call me a visionary, but what is that? It is someone who can see things that others cannot. Our imagination enables us to see and create something that is completely new. It is like throwing all our memories, ideas, thoughts, and wishes into the air, and then seeing what new, unique patterns they make upon landing, just like a kaleidoscope. There are limits to our imagination as imagining is limited to the confines of our experience, memory and knowledge. What we call *imagining* is rarely an unconscious act, since what we imagine is within the images of our mind. Entering the unknown i.e., that which is beyond the scope of our knowledge and experience, requires what I call *Direct Knowing.*

Direct Knowing is perhaps the most difficult to explain because it goes beyond imagining and therefore cannot be explained by means of language, experience, memory or reasoning. Ironically, what we can say about direct knowing is based on common sense, a sense of knowing that some call a *gut feeling*. The only problem with common sense these days, is that it is no longer common! In our relentless drive to amass money and material wealth, we have focused on the physical world of forms at the cost of ignoring the spiritual, invisible world. We've become experts at measuring quantity, and quantity based knowledge is respectable, unlike the qualitative, unproved hunch.

Direct Knowing is not as ridiculous as it sounds. We often have visions, dreams, premonitions or the same ideas at the same time. When I was a boy, I often heard my mother's voice calling me home from miles away. This kind of direct knowing is called telepathy. I have often known what my friends were thinking and received telephone calls shortly after communicating telepathically with them. In the future, I will explain how telepathy works via The Pan Pathways.

One of the most successful experiments in telepathy was

conducted in 1937 by Hubert Wilkins, an Arctic explorer and Harold Sherman, a journalist in New York. Both men were believers in telepathy and agreed to try a long distance test. Three nights a week at 11.30 pm, New York time, Wilkins would go over the events of the day in his mind. Three thousand miles away Sherman would try to pick up his thoughts. Whilst radio communication only managed to contact Wilkins in the Arctic thirteen times in five months, Sherman picked up messages weekly and logged even minor occurrences.

The ancient texts are riddled with cases of direct knowing. It appears that until a few thousand years ago, humans were more open to direct knowing. In recent years there has been an emergence of the phenomenon referred to as E.S.P. (Extra Sensory Perception). All E.S.P. means is, 'the ability to perceive beyond the five senses'. Some call this the sixth sense, which I believe is the result of being in tune with our intuitive nature. The way to regain the skill of direct knowing is to believe it is possible. Faith, intuition and the choice to receive messages are the secret. I discovered The Pan Pathways via the channel of direct knowing.

The Soul! What is it? The soul remains one of the most unknown elements of a human being. We tend not to acknowledge the existence of our soul, as we don't know what it is and if it can be experienced now.

The soul lives in the heart of every living being.

The soul of a human being is for linking the physical and spiritual world. A human being is a physical and spiritual being and a soul resides within us. The soul is the spiritual identity of a human being. The 'I' in 'I am'. The 'I' which chooses what to think, speak and do. That is why the soul is also referred to as the self or spirit. Whatever you call the 'I', we are all beings with soul. The soul of a human being therefore, is spiritually responsible for its condition. If your soul is influenced by the realm of illusion then you will live in a condition of delusion, running from pillar to post. *We call these lost souls.* The soul which is guided by the realm of reality, lives in a condition of being at one with The Infinite Being, God.

When you devote your body and soul to God, it is the union of a human being with The Infinite Being: I am that I am. When this happens, your soul has been illuminated by The Ways of Knowing. The purpose of Knowing is to help the soul reunite with God. The Pathway of Knowing connects the soul of a human being to The Infinite Being – the origin of one's own soul. In every living being, there is a 'knowing of one's own soul'. Humans have the capacity to acknowledge their soul and become soulful as opposed to soulless, that is, when we ignore the soul.

Try this: take this book with you into a play ground or a play school for infants. Read *The Way of Being*, especially the way to separate illusion from reality (pages 110–119). As you feel at one with your Being, look into the faces of the children. You will feel *soul-ful*. Although each child is different, what makes them all the same is their soulful existence. Hence the saying, *'all people are born equal'*. You don't have to suffer, pay penance, cross deserts and wait for judgement day to be soulful.

You can feel soulful now.

The N.E.W.S.

When I was a boy, I was fascinated by new ideas, experiences, people and places. Everything I learned seemed wonderful: so many sights, sounds, places, and people. It was all new, and at the same time I was becoming aware of what was happening in the world. The 'big picture' was revealing itself to me. The one common theme of conversation in all these countries was The News. Almost everyone I met talked about issues related to The News, so I bought myself a small radio and listened carefully to the news everyday. After a while *I too* began to discuss issues which were broadcast on the latest news: earthquakes, murder, civil war, corruption, who won the world cup or a story of another Nazi war criminal who had been hunted down.

As I grew into adulthood, I realised that such discussions had nothing to do with my immediate reality and were in fact making my life miserable. Whenever I saw the news, read the newspaper, watched just about any film, it was being ingrained into my psyche time and time again, just what a terrible world we lived in. Not *knowing* any difference as a teenager, I had believed what I was told and began to view the world according to:

The News!

Later I realised how my view of the world had affected my lifestyle, career friends and family. I had become hard, rough and tough because I thought it necessary. Don't all young people have to prepare themselves to "take on" the world? Teenagers are very impressionable. The television tells them what the world is doing. I see people bombarded by horrific images every hour, often the same story again and again, until we have learnt it like a lesson. This would not be so bad if the stories were good or at least a balance of good and bad. Children see pictures on the news that

150

they would not be allowed to see in a cinema. Whole families eat their dinner between six and seven o'clock whilst watching the most extreme forms of horror our world has to offer. Is it surprising that our youth are behaving in such unethical and immoral ways?

Why are we so addicted to TV NEWS?

Human beings are naturally curious, and we want to have new information, and to be able to witness interesting events. *This is exciting*. People are addicted to television drama, because it enables them to escape their current condition. Television companies know this and consequently, we now have television channels which broadcast NEWS and commercials twenty-four hours a day. The next time you turn on the television, observe which channel you choose first, especially if you want to pass a few minutes whilst having a drink or snack. The NEWS is a quick fix!

Because of the NEWS, we know what is happening on the other side of the world, but how much do we know about the activities in our local community? Whilst a live shoot out, or a murder trial may be thrilling, how does this information enhance the quality of our lives and that of our families? How many hours a day do we sit in front of a television, and what kind of information is going into our minds? The entire human population is tuning into the NEWS on the global news networks. These channels of information are directing our evolution by influencing *the mental condition* and transforming billions of individual minds each day.

The television and, in particular, the NEWS bring us new information. Information is the food of the human psyche. The information which enters our psyche, positive or negative, determines how we use our knowledge. The next time you watch the news, movies and commercials, take note of the motivation of the individuals who are participating in the event. You will find that the realm of illusion plays a dominant role. But what can you do? Beware of the information, illusions which enter your psyche in subtle ways, for the effects are profound.

We are continually being shown the very extremes our race has to offer. Why? The extreme excites the brain like a drug. Most people live dull boring lives and rely on fixes to make life interesting. The media knows this and uses violence, sex, crime, opulence, poverty, and so on in every broadcast. One of the main reasons that people do not involve themselves in local activities is because of the uncaring perceptions the news gives us. We then feel hopeless and helpless. There is a direct connection between what we see and what we do. Quietly observe the reactions of your friends and family when they watch the news.

I don't believe the human race is wicked and uncaring, thoughtless and violent. If you believe this, then you will have to behave defensively or aggressively every time you are reminded of it by the wickedness of others. You will in fact become wicked yourself. I am not saying that there is no wickedness in our world. Yes, we have wars, rape, violence, destruction and disease, but if we focus on them all the time, then that is what we shall procreate. We need a balanced view of the world and that may mean either looking for good news or not watching the news for a while. You see, all information enters into the subconscious which does not know the difference between time and place. The subconscious mind thinks the news is your/its reality and sends signals to the mind and body. That is why we get affected by horror stories in our living room and even have nightmares.

The mind is like laundry, which has to be washed and aired otherwise it stinks. Try a television or a news fast for a week. Don't watch television, listen to the radio or read the newspapers for a week and then see how you feel. Take a walk down the street, look at the notice board in your local library and find out what is happening in your own community. Find out if the world *you live in* is as violent and uncaring as the news makes it out to be. Make your own news, by doing something positive for your community.

Which Way?

I was once a homeless street kid, travelling into oblivion. Being alone, there was no one to tell me what to think or do. Unknowingly, I listened to my intuition which is the source of my fortune. Intuition has provided me with the clarity, and direction to overcome all manner of challenges.

Intuition has awakened me.

At the age of fourteen my mother died and I had a choice: to stay where I was or to begin a journey of discovery. Then as a young man, I was faced with another crossroads. The choice had been to join a monastery or the Royal Marine Commandos. Those, and many other choices based on Intuition, have brought me here… my life is paradise.

I have had many demonstrations of the power of intuition in my life. One of the most memorable was on the 1st of August '95. I was invited to spend a summer on a farm in Normandy, France. It was a beautiful, clear evening and a polo game was in progress. On the edge of the field, a woman called Pauline was instructing Eugénie, a girl of nine, on how to ride. As the little girl galloped past where I was sitting I sensed fear. Soon the horse was in full gallop and I gave chase. At a distance I saw her fall.

By the time I had reached her, some ten seconds had lapsed and she lay motionless with her head in a distorted position. There was no breath, no pulse and checking her eyes, clearly she had been knocked unconscious on impact and her lungs had collapsed. I had a dilemma. To give her mouth to mouth, I had to move her head away from her chest, which would kill her if the spine had been severed on impact. The question was: *which way* do I move her body, and how far? Going on my intuition, I moved her head far enough to give her mouth to mouth resuscitation. Within two minutes she had started to breathe by herself. She had broken all her ribs, her collar bone on the left side and had punctured a lung. It was a miracle that Eugénie was alive. No matter how impossible the challenge appears, through intuition you will know the solution. In a world of chaos and darkness, we can find our way with intuition. Intuition is the ultimate compass to navigate by.

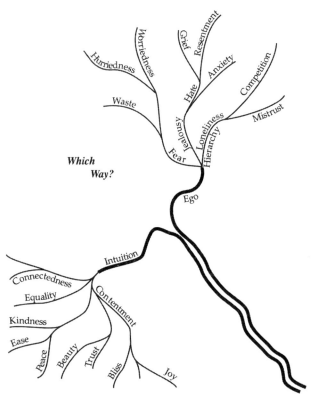

Every day and at each moment, there is a fork in your life. You are at such a fork now. Now is the appointed time. Listen to your intuition and it will take you on a magical path, where miracles shall follow miracles and wonders shall never cease.

The Power of Patience

When I was a boy, my mother would often say to me, *"drop by drop lakes are created"*, which is a very old proverb of Sanskrit origin. Then, in my teenage years when I was travelling through Rome, I saw on the Vatican wall, an old emblem saying, *"Festina Lente"* which in Latin means *"Go fast, slowly"*. Intuitively I knew what these words meant, for I felt their power in my body and yet, as I grew up into manhood, I slowly and gradually forgot my mother's words and the power they brought to me.

Over the next decade I embarked on big projects that required immense effort, which drained me to the point of exhaustion. I had become powerless and the cause was impatience. I had, in fact, become a puppet of the fast moving, instant world we live in – a clatter of noises and senseless actions. Not only had I become powerless due to my impatience, it was humiliating to observe myself try to cover up my stupidity by behaving patiently.

The truth was my impatience had eaten away at the core of my being and all the knowledge and wisdom I had in my head was useless. The way forward was simple. I had to be more patient. To do that meant giving up all that was making me impatient. It was a Catch 22 situation. I was powerless within, because of my lack of patience, and I would be powerless without if I let go of these projects. Either way I would end up powerless. Having no choice, I surrendered!

The lack of patience is a lack of wisdom.

Surrendering all forms of power is the most powerful thing we can do. It is the practice of patience in its purest form, that gives us access to the absolute power of wisdom. Without patience there can be no wisdom and hence no power. This is why patience is one of the most important elements in our lives. Patience gives us the wisdom to choose wisely and the power to change the face of events. Hence the proverb, *"Patience is a virtue"*! The more patient we become, the less we force ourselves and others to achieve. We simply live and let live and everything falls into place as if by magic.

Patience makes everything possible.

The practice of patience is very powerful, for it makes everything possible. No matter what it is we want to do, the moment we apply patience, it is guaranteed to happen sooner rather than later. Most people fail to achieve what they set out to do because they give up or self-destruct by going too fast. The following example provides valuable insight into the practice and power of patience.

> The Chinese bamboo is planted and must be watered every day. A week, two weeks, a month, two months and three months go by and nothing happens. Four months, five months and six months and still nothing happens. Then, after six months, during a period of six weeks, it grows from seed to twenty-eight feet!

In the same way, the discovery and development of HELP has taken twenty-eight years of trials and testings. The word *patience* means constancy and continuance. In Sanskrit they say, *"the fruits of patience are very sweet."* The James I Bible says, *"be joyful when you fall into diverse kinds of trials and testings, knowing that the trying of your faith brings out patience."*

Shakespeare said, *"To climb steep hills requires slow pace at first."* The central message of all these examples is that patience is a virtue that makes everything possible, be it learning to play a sport or a musical instrument, bringing up children, finding a cure for a disease, or bringing peace and prosperity to the world. Patience makes the impossible possible, and doing the impossible is to have the wisdom to make miracles. All miracles have one thing in common. They are not forced.

Knowing in Practice

Every day we learn something new. Every idea, thought and feeling we have, was once new to us. The human mind has a limitless capacity to learn new things, for example, from birth to the age of eighteen we learn to eat, walk, play games, talk, dance, name colours, people and places, ride a bicycle, make friends, learn languages, study mathematics, history, biology and chemistry. Where has our miraculous ability to learn so many things actually got us? When we look at the lives of 'learned people', what do we see? We see a jumble of ideas, information and tradition. A lot of people amass knowledge as if it were, money or materials.

Knowledge is dead. Knowing is alive.

Knowledge comes from the accumulation of information, whilst Knowing comes from actually living. Knowledge is past, fixed and dead, whilst Knowing is current, constant and alive. Knowledge comes from past memory, whereas Knowing comes from the moment. *Now,* is the only reality, and Knowing enables us to keep moving and flowing with what is living and happening, now. If you are using knowledge to live you will suffer, because you cannot reduce reality to a static state or thing and then use knowledge to reach truth, life and reality. They are moving and flowing constantly, hence if you are using knowledge to live, you will not be able *to be*, with what is happening now. With Knowing you are *alive and living*, because life is constantly moving and changing.

The Pathway of Knowing will help you to discover the source of your knowing, where all your knowing has come from. Through Knowing, you will discover who you are, what you are, what you know, and how you feel. Learn to trust your Knowing.

The knowledge that we posses is exactly that, possession, and as such, we can become very attached to knowledge we have in our mind or the knowledge of our children. What is education? Knowledge is a storage of information, whilst Knowing is free flowing from moment to moment, choosing the best direction and course of action.

> To practise The Way of Knowing, you must let go of all knowledge and inwardly die. Then you will be living openly, and become receptive to your 'knowingness'. Let this knowingness guide your ideas, thoughts, feelings and actions into the world. Imagine your Knowing, flowing like a river from a source deep within you, and that you are moving, flowing and bathing in knowingness. All that you see, feel and touch appears new, neutral and without prejudice.

As you follow your Knowing, you will *wake up* to new realities, that we call *the unknown*. Many people ask me what it is like to be faced with the unknown constantly. Going into the unknown feels like walking away from everything you have believed and loved. To give you an idea of what it feels like, go to an open field. Close your eyes and clasp your hands behind your head. Now walk in any direction and you will get a glimpse of the unknown. Going into the unknown can be very difficult. The human mind is fixed and fears the realm of reality. To enter the unknown, the mind has to learn to look at life anew.

When we were born, *everything* was new, but our minds had the freedom, without fear, to encounter all that we saw without prior knowledge. That is Knowing in action. The new born is connected to its knowingness and does not rely on knowledge to survive against all odds. We live in a world where knowledge is supposed to be power. Is it really? If so, where are the really powerful people? I have met people who have encyclopedic knowledge of science, philosophy, theology, politics and technology, but lack the very substance of being human. Have you ever wondered why a new born looks so powerful? It is because living is a natural state of Knowing. The Way of Knowing links our lives with that natural source of knowing: the Direct Knowing that comes from our Being and ultimately from The Infinite Being.

The
Pathway
of

Relating

Reflections on Relating

I have a variety of satisfying relationships.

I freely give and receive love and support.

I enjoy touching and sharing physical and spiritual contact with others.

I am comfortable with the feminine and masculine aspects of myself.

I have meaningful relationships with people of all ages including children and elders.

I am in harmony and share affection with the people I work with.

I feel a deep respect for my friends and family.

I am free from fear and guilt and am completely honest with myself and others.

I am free from revengeful thoughts and actions.

I have realised that lying equals dying.

I know how to transform conflict creatively.

I treat with respect everyone I meet, the rich and the poor, wise and foolish, black or white, male or female, etc.

I know how to handle resistance from people wisely.

I can remain honest and centred in the midst of deception and treachery.

I am part of a club or community where I have gained respect for fulfilling my responsibilities over a long period of time.

I take enough time to be alone and nurture myself.

I know how to listen.

I have a positive image of myself and express myself freely.

I am accepting of non-orthodox forms of relationships: homosexuality, bisexuality, celibacy, extended families etc.

I am open to new ways of relating to people, animals and nature.

The Role of Relating

A human being is born every second, and so another living being begins *relating* on the Earth. As soon as we are born, we begin relating through our breathing, feeling, and crying. We naturally expect others to respond to our needs. Just by being in the world you are relating with other people and other life forms, which in turn are relating with you. Relating is a constant, *universal* interaction, not only between living beings, but also of matter, energy and other dimensions of existence. We have night and day, for example, because the Earth is relating to the sun, which in turn is relating to other planets, and so on.

A human being has the capacity to relate on infinite levels, from the smallest particles to multiple universes existing parallel to our own. It is because of the *miraculous* gift of relating that our species has evolved such a vast consciousness. It is by relating that we have discovered metals, minerals, and named life forms, plants and planets. The more we relate, the more conscious we become of our environment on every level of existence. Our capacity for relating has made us the *masters* of the Earth, and all other life forms are seen as *lesser* beings by humans. It is by relating that humans control one another, other life forms and exploit the Earth's resources for our own ends, but is that what relating is for?

What is the purpose of Relating?

Is it to amass wealth, have power over others, produce goods for profit, gain knowledge, enlightenment, or to become famous and immortal? If we don't know what relating is for, then how can we relate to, or for, a purpose that *serves everyone* in each of our relationships? A power hungry person, for instance, cannot see the purpose of relating with other people as equals. A deceitful person cannot see the sense in trust, honour and integrity. Why are we human beings, with all our consciousness, relating in such harmful ways? What propels a person to lie, cheat, abuse, manipulate, kill and conquer? The answer is fear: a fear of life that originates from a way of relating based on the hunter-hunted mentality. The only difference is that now we don't hunt to survive, but to win and gain as much as we can. We call this way of relating, *competition*.

Our whole system is based on competition, which is driven by fear, passed on from the days when our species hunted with clubs and stones. What we call competition, is propelled by the primal fear of hunter-hunted, where the winner survives and the loser dies. Very few of us have grown up in a culture where competition was not the way of relating. This competitive way of relating is so primal that we do not recognise our own participation in promoting competitive culture. We are caught in a social dynamic of one-up, or one-down, that can be a brutal boxing match to decide the winner. It can be so subtle that the shape of your eyes makes you a loser. When that happens, we have used relating to create a pecking order, which has led to hierarchies in our family, society, organisations and nations.

Hierarchies, by their very nature, demean people and turn them against one another. When we compare, we become separated. This can happen at home, work, with our friends, within groups and across countries. Competition breeds, not only winners and losers, but also extremes such as higher and lower, better and worse, beautiful and ugly, desirable and undesirable, etc. How often have we felt superior to others, or felt like a loser in front of our friends and families? We can change these feelings, by changing the way we think of relating. Why should we change a way of relating that our species has used for over two million years? In short, because we have a global crisis on our hands, and the only way to survive and save our natural habitat for future generations, is for us to co-operate on an individual and collective level.

When there is a crisis in our family, we all pull together. We need to apply the same approach globally to overcome the crisis in the family of humanity. Each one of us, in our own way, can help someone each day, by changing our motivation for relating from competition to co-operation. What we can do and what we actually do in our relationships are often poles apart. For example, when people are asked to give blood, they often refuse, even when giving a pint of blood is completely safe. What prevents people from relating in co-operation, and how can we encourage this human trait?

In every act of relating, our minds have been conditioned to compete and so we are faced with the separateness of you and I, them and us, us and nature. All this prevents us from helping. Our aim must be to become one in relating, but how can we change our whole way of relating? If we say faith, love, acceptance, communication, etc., we are giving words not solutions. We must replace the competitive way of relating, with a co-operative way of relating. What we need is a way of relating that is so simple and practical that it can be learnt by every individual.

The Pathway of Relating brings people together as one, not only within humanity, but with creation. Anything that exists belongs to the whole of creation, by definition. The function of The Pathway of Relating is to transform our way of relating from competition to co-operation, so that it serves our species in every relationship. The family of humanity is made up of relationships, and the way you and I relate is very important.

The object of Relating is to show us how to relate and respect the different kinds of life forms, thereby forming a network of relationships all relating to one another. With every human being that comes into our world, we can demonstrate to them how to co-operate from the beginning. For the first things learnt are the hardest to forget, and so The Way of Relating is passed on from one generation to the next.

*The purpose
of Relating is
to help.*

The Way of Relating

The Way of Relating is a way of living in harmony with creation. To live in harmony, we have to understand who we are, where we come from and where we belong. We live on this planet, which is part of the universe believed to have been formed by the big bang. It is estimated that there are a hundred billion galaxies in our universe, which have existed parallel to other multiple universes. The Earth is said to have existed for 4.6 billion solar years. If we compare that with a man of forty-six years of age, then our species first appeared about an hour ago. The life span of a human being compared to the Earth is one second and, in that fleeting moment, we are capable of *relating* with the vastness of creation.

Relating creates vibrations which know no frontiers.

Relating is a very powerful pathway, since everything you relate with sends a vibration throughout your immediate surrounding, as well as throughout the vast network of relationships, which link the natural world. When you clap your hands for example, the sound does not disappear, but merges with sounds from your surroundings. These sounds merge with other sounds and become the *hum* of your city. In the same way, each comet, planet, sun, star, galaxy and universe emits a hum that becomes *one* cosmic vibration.

Our aim is to *feel* this vibration and live accordingly. This vibration is created by every interaction in creation including you and I. Just like musicians in an orchestra playing in accord, we can live in harmony or disharmony with the cosmic vibration. But how can we feel something we are not aware of, let alone live in harmony with it? We begin by building on the understanding that every act of relating sends out a vibration which is carried by what

I call *The Pathway of Relating*. The Pathway of Relating enables us to tap into the cosmic vibration, through the act of relating. This is how it works. Just as we have become oblivious to the hum in our cities, we have grown accustomed to the sound of our footsteps, our breathing and the beating of our hearts. In the same way we have ignored the *sound of relating*, but the moment we become conscious of the act of relating, we can hear and feel the vibration. Are you with me so far?

Every time we relate with anything or anyone, we create a vibration that becomes one with the cosmic vibration. The *whole* of creation is connected by The Pathway of Relating, which carries the cosmic vibration from one object and one entity to another. The vibration I speak of exists within and outside us, but in the humdrum of life we cannot hear it. The Pathway of Relating reveals and reconnects us with the cosmic vibration. By listening, and living according to the vibration of creation, we discover who we are, and where we come from and belong. Just as the drummer and dancer become one with the beat, we live in harmony with the rhythm of creation, via the cosmic vibration.

The Pathway of Relating flows to and through everything in creation.

By following an act of relating back to its origin, we can *sense* the vibration and feel the pulse flowing through us, somewhat like listening to and feeling the pulse and vibration of our own hand. In this way we can connect with anything to which we relate. Once we can hear and feel the pulse, we can tune ourselves to live in harmony, just as we do with the rhythm of day and night. When this happens, we are relating and living in harmony with creation.

To do this we must align ourselves and our relationships with creation, by learning *The Way of Relating*. To that end, I shall present The Ways of Relating which will enable individuals to form harmonious relationships. The basic dynamic of relationships is as follows:

Help brings harmony.

Harm brings discord.

To use an extreme example, all wars are caused by the fear of harm, whereas harmony comes from wanting to help. The very idea of helping someone, makes us feel in harmony with them and thus we form harmonious relationships with each other, other life forms and the Earth.

An act of relating is either helpful or harmful and creates a vibration that goes into the world, multiplies and comes back many fold to its creator. The vibration we send is the *cause* that has an actual *effect* and comes back to us in the form of helpful or harmful events. Each one of us is relating to something or someone, all the time, but how aware are we of the vibration we are creating? Relating is a natural activity, but when we use it consciously, it can change the course of our lives and influence the world in miraculous ways.

What makes The Pathway of Relating so powerful?

It is the force which flows via the Pathway, that makes Relating so powerful. The Pathway of Relating channels the force of creation, to and from us. We can use this force to manifest whatever we wish. This is how it works. By relating you send out a vibration, that is just like planting a seed that grows and bears fruit a hundred fold. The Pathway of Relating is governed by this law of cause and effect or *come back* with every act of relating, be it helpful or harmful. That is why Jesus helped those who despised and attacked him.

Imagine how much harmony and prosperity we can bring to our lives if we *'planted the seed of HELP'* with every act of relating? When I first started to discover The Way of HELP, I had neither work, money nor a home, but I had the power of Relating, which is free. The act of relating in order to help humanity and the Earth has come back to me in the form of harmony, prosperity and The HELP Programme, which in turn is founded on the simple act of help. The HELP book is the result of the same process of planting and nurturing a seed, which grows, bears fruit and multiplies.

Imagine how fruitful our efforts would be if we could use relating for the sole purpose of helping. Imagine how much harmony and prosperity we could bring by *'sowing the seeds of HELP'*. If we look at humanity as a tree, then the fruits of our labour have been denied or have tasted bitter. Each one of us belongs to the tree of humanity and the way we are relating has a comeback, not only to you and me, but on the entire tree. When we look at a tree, its harmony is portrayed in the way it is *relating* to its surroundings.

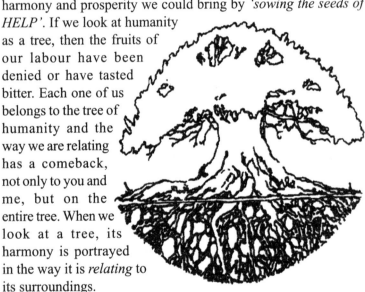

Each part of the tree is helping the whole tree.

The roots provide water and stability, the trunk holds it upright while the branches nurture the leaves which absorb the sunlight. The tree bears fruit because it is helping itself via The Pathway of Relating.

In the same way, the act of relating begins by us relating to ourselves, through thoughts, feelings, aspirations and actions. The way we relate to ourselves, is the way we relate with the world at large. We tend to think that we are separate, and that is why we help ourselves, but harm others. We do not realise that we are all one *tree*. For example, how do people relate to others in church? Now compare that with the way we are relating in our homes, street, society etc. The Pathway of Relating is a way of relating in harmony, in *every* interaction.

Every human relationship sends a vibration across the whole tree of life. Just like the pulse of our heartbeat, each act of relating vibrates across the body of humanity. Many people want to participate in creating a better world, but feel unable and powerless, whilst others campaign against the status quo or plot revolutions. We have to understand that the power to create a better world is *within* us. The way we relate to others right now can send shock waves across the whole of humanity. You don't have to be a leader, visionary or a revolutionary to bring harmony and prosperity to humanity. By simply relating to help those you are with, you will be making the most helpful and fruitful contribution. This means nurturing your personal and professional relationships, as you would a tree, for the better they are cared for the better they will grow.

People seem to think that relationships grow by themselves and that they don't need to be nurtured. Relationships are such an integral part of human existence that we have a tendency to take them for granted. How many people ever stop to think, really think, about their relationships: what they amount to, how they are developed and how to create harmonious ones? We adopt a consumer attitude to our relationships, "If this one isn't right, I will get a new one!" Most people, as a result, deny themselves the attainable joy of the deep satisfaction that wholehearted commitment can bring through truly intimate relationships.

Sound information about making the most of relationships, is usually hard to acquire and many of us learn about relationships simply by having them. We learn the hard way, by repeated trial and error. In time, we come to what is usually the central, most important partnership of adult life, an enduring and fulfilling relationship and we are often ill-prepared for it. Everywhere we look, we see troubled and torn relationships. Often adults with relationship problems do not talk about them with others who could help them or learn from their experience. Is it surprising that the most common problems that people seek counselling for, are substance abuse and relationship problems?

Ironically, it is loneliness, and a deep need for belonging, that drives the most capable people to substance abuse. Others feel disconnected from the vast society they live in, while hoping to meet like-minded people through a chance meeting on a bus, train or plane. As our societies have grown in scale, the traditional community ties have weakened, as have the individual's means of supportive relationships.

When I was living in London I met an elderly cockney man who told me what it was like to live in the Old Kent Road. He told me how people helped each other and about harvest thanksgiving when the street was like a fairground. He talked about neighbours and the trust between people. The one thing I still remember from that conversation is when he said, *"we was all one"*. Then came the war and people got separated, buildings were pulled down and all his friends moved away. I could see that he was lonely and looking back at old times, whilst yearning for human contact. To think that he is now sitting in front of a television, watching hundreds of people, but without a friend is very sad.

We all need close friends and at least one very intimate companion, but making friends is not easy, especially as people have become isolated and cautious of 'strangers' in society. Who do you trust? Who is your friend? We must understand that we are all strangers, until we make friends. In order for us to start relating fully, we need to open our hearts and minds to *fully experience* the event of meeting people and seeing new places. The more open we are with ourselves, the more open we are to life. The problem begins when we close ourselves to the world and become disconnected from The Ways of Relating. The fact is *nothing* can live in isolation and the more we try to, the more we suffer. Relating is being totally open, letting go and leaving our comfort zone so that we no longer resist relating to the world.

When I was travelling across Europe and Asia, there were many opportunities to meet new people, experience strange places and relate to the elements, because I was living out in the open. During these years I learnt a lot about people, animals and the elements of the Earth. People often find it easier to make new friends on holiday, when they are in hospital or in a crisis because they are *open*. Opening oneself is like dying, just as a seed must die to become a plant. Opening our hearts and minds allows us to meet people and relate to the world wholeheartedly. Relating wholeheartedly sounds very appealing, but how can we create these experiences and relationships? Is there *a way* to living wholeheartedly and harmoniously, and if so, can this wisdom be passed on from one person to another?

The Way of Relating relies on a process which works in a cycle of constant renewal in our relationships. All relationships change and evolve constantly. If we are to have fulfilling relationships, we must flow with the cycle of renewal as it occurs, but how do we do that and where do we begin? Let me ask you a simple question to assess your understanding of Relating:

How does the process of Relating work?

Simple as it is, most people do not have a clue of how the process of Relating actually works. Is it any wonder that broken relationships cause so much disunity on every level of our society?

Pan Pathways: The evolutionary spiral of Relating.

The spiral of Relating will enable individuals to connect with The Pathway of Relating and flow with the process. This process will help you to initiate new relationships, solve problems and bring harmony to every act of relating. Although the main focus is on practical ways of enriching personal relationships, the same process can be applied between groups and organisations.

The spiral of Relating is an ongoing process and these four stages are active in every relationship throughout our lives. Choose any relationship and work out where you are and what needs nurturing. The way you have been relating with other people, life forms and the Earth has come back to you like a cycle of events.

A relationship is a living thing and, just like every living thing, it has a cycle. If we are to *understand* what is happening in our relationships, we need to know how they work and how to develop them. There are infinite activities or interactions that form relationships, yet there are four stages that seem to appear in all realms of human interplay. *Meeting, Investigation, Intimacy* and *Integration*, play off each other to create a continuum we call life.

Meeting is the first stage of any relationship, be it with a dog, dolphin or person. The initial contact or initiation with something or someone new is a very mysterious happening, for so many different events, decisions, and influences have brought us to the point of meeting. Some people call it chance or luck, fate or fortune, synchronicity or destiny.

Is it by chance that you are reading this book?

Whatever it is, the potential of a new encounter with another has enormous power and the way we use it can lead us to prosperity or poverty. This is why we say *"first impressions are lasting impressions"*, for what happens between us in the initial milliseconds is connected to our deepest thoughts, feelings and preferences. When we meet someone for the first time, we have ventured into the unknown. Going into the unknown triggers off all kinds of reactions and responses as we try to make head or tail of who or what we are dealing with. For example, how do you cope with meeting people for the first time?

What makes you choose this person rather than that one? Something about the person attracted you. Attraction between people is the first stage of Relating, whether it is friendship, business or sexual. We speak of chemistry, of some mysterious force like magnetism that draws some people together just as it repels others. On the whole, we have a tendency to label people according to their colour, creed, clothing or career, but is that all that we are? We all believe we want to be attractive, yet what is it that attracts? Is it something in the person you meet or something in yourself?

People give off subtle signals constantly, sending messages with body language or dress, but these have to be received in order for attraction to take place. In other words you have to be looking for something in order to see it! So attraction is as much about your needs and desires as about the other person's qualities. Much of what we think we want from our relationships is social garbage, the psycho-babble of mass media. Taoists say, *"Desire can never be satisfied."* No matter how much you eat, you'll always feel hungry again later. Your desires are frequently either manufactured by media, culture and convention or they are false trails leading you to frustration. What you want isn't necessarily the same as what you need.

Our ears clamour with wants, but need speaks in a quiet voice. Relationships fail because needs aren't met and because we lack the knowledge of our own and other's needs. You may think you want a partner who looks like a model and has a lifestyle of a high-flyer, but you may need gentleness, humour and inspiration. We act like consumers, shopping in the human supermarket for the latest life accessory, dazzled by the hype, the superficial, the novel, the tasty luxurious titbits, ending up with a malnourished heart, starved of the basic nourishment of relationships and love.

The first meeting is a highly charged event, which can change the direction of your life *forever*. One person can make you more fortunate in life than having a thousand friends. *How can you meet such a person in such a vast and fast moving world?*

The next time you are walking across a street, shopping mall or a subway, open your mind and be aware that very powerful forces are at work in bringing you very close to those you should meet. Take courage and make contact. This is how I met Vaughan Hawthorne-Nelson, who helped to create the HELP book.

Investigation is the second stage, where we begin to explore the nature of our relationships, lying below or beyond the surface of our persona. We start to look a little bit closer... and closer! With the investigation process, there appear to be three main depths that form the 'pool' of the human condition.

The first is superficial, where we find out each other's homes, jobs, tastes in music, etc. The second is usually hidden from most and only a few select individuals are privileged to enter that depth, and even then they cannot stay there. This is where we keep our hidden agendas, phobias and fantasies.

The third, the deepest part of the person, is usually out of bounds and no one, including oneself, is allowed to enter this space. All kinds of memories in the form of fears, phobias, pain and resentments are at the bottom of the pool. As we get older, the junk at the bottom of the pool increases and we become masters at laying decoys to keep people from investigating this part of the pool. My question is: what have we done that is so bad that we cannot let others know about it? Before all the junk was ditched there, what else existed there and is it buried underneath layer after layer of personal and societal garbage?

In all these years of working with people, I have never come across a person whose 'bad actions' even remotely outweighed the 'good ones'! Even the lives of the most tyrannical despots, when investigated on a day-to-day basis, portray kindness, joy, humility and compassion to their loved ones.

Our hearts are like our homes and we need the company of others to feel loved. People who live behind *closed doors* have been hurt and that pain in their hearts prevents them from being open, spontaneous and intimate, even with their loved ones. Talk with yourself, pray and ask God to help you. Let God into your heart and others will follow.

Intimacy is the next stage in the Relating process. Let me clarify what I understand from my experience of intimacy. My definition of intimacy is 'seeing and feeling without thinking', for the moment I think about what I see and what I feel, I stop being intimate. The nature of the mind is to think about things, about what we see and feel. Intimacy is about feeling and about being. Thought takes us one step away from being, it makes us evaluate and think about it. Consequently, we are always one step away from being intimate. So if I want to be intimate with you and I want to hug you, if I think about hugging you... then I think about hugging you! Intimacy is not about thinking of giving you a hug, it's about hugging you, that's what makes the experience intimate.

The lack of intimacy in any form of relationship is the central cause of breakdown. As soon as we get close to someone, something prevents us from being intimate. Why? The fear of feeling loved. Intimacy creates intense feelings of love which can be so overwhelming that we sabotage or avoid the possibility of intimacy. Is there a lack of intimacy in your life?

In our relationships we always look for different kinds of intimacy, such as physical, mental and spiritual intimacy. All of us want to connect with our partners, parents and friends on an intimate level, yet thinking prevents us from doing so. When you see a chance to be intimate, take it. If you're thinking, you will keep thinking forever. Simply approach the person and say, *"Do you know what fear is? Well, I am afraid now because I'd like to give you a hug",* and then do it! The most versatile channel of intimacy I know is a hug. You can hug in any and all relationships, from a friend, your father or mother, sister or brother, your teacher or a tree, your president or your guru.

The good thing about hugging is that it brings people so close to each other that you can't actually see one another's 'faults'! When we hug someone, for a few seconds we loose ourselves and become one. The best example of intimacy I can think of is that between a mother and child. The love that is generated radiates outward, making other people feel intimate.

Integration is the final stage in the cycle of Relating. As we have seen, when two people meet, they investigate and come close to each other, and finally integrate each other's character. People are like revolving entities in time and space. They are like squares, triangles, hexagons, pentagons and as they come close to each other, the edges touch or hit and produce certain sounds like Ooch, Awh, Pow, Wham, Ooh, Aahh, Mmhh! Every time the shapes meet each other, an edge gets chipped off part of the ego. Sometimes the collisions are too much and we need time and space to recover. As the process of Relating continues, the entities become rounder and ultimately both revolve in harmony.

By harmony, I mean the capacity to get on with each other and not behave like a fart doesn't stink! If our understanding of harmonious relationships is that of 'nicey-nicey', without disagreements, we shall never learn and grow as human beings, Relating in a real sense. There are always going to be disagreements which are part of the integration process. There is often frustration prior to total integration, because we cannot break through or relate fully, due to reasons still unknown. Sooner or later though, we start to feel things *coming together* in our relationships, where two become one and then become two again.

Integration is a critical step of any relationship, for the failure to do so results in disharmony. The ego often gets in the way for becoming *one* with another represents a threat to one's identity. This is why integration leads to transformation. Evolution has relied heavily on integration, as a means of perpetuating life, from the dawn of creation. If we look at nature, every atom, molecule, element and creature somehow manage to get on with each other.

Integration requires a delicate balance between removing barriers between yourself and others, and maintaining healthy boundaries for your own individual identity. False integration occurs when we *fall* in love, i.e., when we deny ourselves in the relationship. To hide inside a relationship is self-denial and this stunts the growth of both partners: we are merely projecting our desires onto our partner and ignoring the reality of who or what they are. To falsely perceive another as part of us denies their freedom of will, their freedom to grow. True integration honours and nurtures individuality, it promotes the spiritual growth of the other person. When you do that to someone else, you automatically do it to yourself too. Both parties grow and evolve through interdependency.

Competition to Co-operation

As you put the information and insights gained from this book into practice, you too are becoming part of a new era and a new breed of human being. In choosing to read this book, you have in fact affirmed your willingness to change from competitive (hunter-hunted) to a co-operative (helper-helped) approach towards relating with the outside world.

This process may take several years to complete on an individual level and will most certainly be no less challenging than climbing Mount Everest without oxygen. In moving from competition to co-operation you may encounter resistance, not only from within yourself, but also from your family, friends and colleagues. Why? In choosing to trade competition (win-lose) for co-operation (win-win), you are not only going against the current flow of society, but also directing the psyche of humanity into the unknown. Going into the unknown, even if it is for the better, brings all kinds of fears and phobias to the fore. For millions of years the human psyche has relied on competition as a means for survival. It will not let go of it easily.

It is only by understanding the need for change and the way to achieve it, that we will be able to promote and make the transition. Whilst competition has been necessary so far in our evolution, we have now reached a point where co-operation is becoming the means for survival. Over the past hundred thousand years, we have learnt to couple intelligence with competition. We have in fact mastered the art of competition to the nth degree, and control our whole environment, where winners get everything and losers nothing. This process is wiping out thirty-five species of life every month, killing over one-hundred and twenty million people through starvation and making two hundred million people homeless every year! Humanity is at war with itself and the Earth. War is the ultimate outcome of competition. *"Surely competition is healthy?"* Some may say so, but is it really?

Firstly, competition by its very nature, results in haves and have-nots, which results in life for some and death for others. This brutal conflict can only continue for so long, until there is anarchy. The threat of nuclear war may be over, but anarchy on an unprecedented level is a real possibility, that is, unless each one of us makes the transition from competition to co-operation.

Secondly, as more and more individuals make the transition, there also exists the possibility of a violent reaction from the status quo, albeit delivered by *the hidden hand.* Co-operation, by its very nature, results in a more equal distribution of land, wealth, resources and power. Those who have come to control so much of our current world culture, have done so by mastering the art of war (competition), passed on from generation to generation. In the past these people have been dislodged from their positions by means of revolution. The drawback with revolution is that the poor always remain poor, regardless of the change in power.

Our aim must be evolution not revolution. By becoming aware of the need for a transition from competition to co-operation, we shall avert anarchy, war and revolution. Even those now in power will see the sense in this. This is not to say that there will be no reaction or resistance, as we move from the old to the new, but since evolution is slower and often unseen, it will provoke less direct conflict. Less resistance will make the transition more manageable, smoother and faster. The secret of social change is to initiate changes slowly and quietly, without an axe to grind.

One who has an axe to grind, has an axe.

As you apply the content of this book, be aware that you are becoming a pioneer of social change and a new breed of human being. As such, you may unknowingly provoke those around you. I suggest that in the early stages of your transition, you stay away from the sceptics and the cynics, instead, seek like-minded people who will help you adapt to the new way.

Forgiveness and Acceptance

From the moment of waking in the morning until going to sleep at night, there are moments in the day in which you consciously or unconsciously recall memories from yesterday, last week, last month, and so on, right back to your very first impression of life in the womb. In fact, everything that has happened to you has been stored in your memory which then influences your judgement of people and the conditions you create.

To use an extreme example: Hitler judged the Jews according to his memory of the Jewish people and look at the condition he created. In the same way, the way we judge others is based on our memory. But what has our memory and judgement got to do with forgiveness?

Forgiveness is the way we 'wipe the slate clean' of hurt, hate, abuse, blame and punishment. Without forgiveness, you would not have a friend, only foes. That is why forgiveness has played a part in all spiritual paths to reinstate harmony in human relationships. How often do you need to forgive or be forgiven by your family, friends, workmates and strangers?

Is there anyone you are trying to forgive?

If so, why? What I am going to say may be difficult to accept, because forgiveness has its roots in judgement. *The way* you judge determines whether or not you need to forgive. Let me explain. If your life is based on the realm of illusion, your judgement will cause hurt, hate and fighting, only to be resolved by forgiving.

The need to forgive or be forgiven is caused by judgement, based on the realm of illusion. Think about it! Let go of the illusions in favour of reality and you will no longer need to *fight and forgive.* Instead you will accept the way they are. What is the difference

181

between forgiveness and acceptance? Forgiveness is rooted in illusion and acceptance is based on reality.

How do we move from forgiveness to acceptance? The next time you are trying to forgive someone, look at the realm of illusion* and see why you are judging that person. For example, If you have been cheated with money, then the illusion of *gain and loss* is the judgment you are tying to forgive. By accepting *neutrality* as the reality, you will accept what has happened and will not need to forgive. In this way, you can work through illusion into reality and free yourself from the trap of judgement and forgiveness. As your focus in life changes from illusion to reality, the need to 'fight and forgive' will diminish and in time disappear altogether. When that happens, your judgement of others will be without prejudice.

When the judgement born of hate, resentment, guilt, jealously or malice dies, there is nothing and nobody to forgive. For instance, what would happen if the Jews did not even try to forgive the Germans for the Holocaust? How much more love would we have in our hearts if we did not use a single thought on judging and forgiving those who have *done us wrong*?

Acceptance is holding no one in bondage, whatever their sins, wanting no vengeance and no revenge, but only to embrace and serve wholeheartedly. Is that not the nature of God? Then is it not a contradiction to ask God to forgive you? God accepts you the way you are and does not need to forgive you!

Forgiveness is man made. Acceptance is divine.

So why is forgiveness so commonly practised in religion? Because the illusions are so deeply rooted in human judgement that forgiveness has become spiritual law. From here on, face the reality of your judgement and live in acceptance.

* See page 113.

Overcoming Resistance

To cut a long story short, human evolution has been preoccupied with the fight between good versus evil. The aim of this fighting has supposedly been to preserve, promote and create a better, safer and more beautiful world. In essence to create *Paradise on Earth.* Over thousands of years, we have mastered the way of fighting. We have taken the brutal act of combat and developed it to the ultimate degree. To this day, the forces of good and evil continue to fight, confront and campaign against each other. Who is actually winning? Can anyone really win? Is it necessary and if not, what other ways do we have to create a better world?

First we shall explore the three ways that our species have used to overcome resistance and then I shall propose a fourth: The Way of Absence. Each individual and organisation must choose the means necessary in order to achieve the goal. The goal, whatever that is, will to a large extent determine which one of the four ways is applicable. Out of the four ways, there is no better or worse, right or wrong, only the consequences of the way used.

The first is **fighting against the opposing force.** This could mean anything, from a shouting match to secret campaigns, to sabotage or overthrow the enemy. The use of force, brutal or subtle, has been the instrument used to conclude most disputes in the history of humanity. The question is: where has all that fighting and campaigning brought us? The fact is, conditions on the Earth are unbearable and are getting worse! Although fighting has been the most widely used system of social reform, is it possible that it has served its purpose and is now hindering progress?

The second approach to overcoming opposing forces is **non co-operation,** otherwise referred to as 'fighting without fighting'. It is still a means of fighting but more subtle in its delivery. This system of social reform was used by Gandhi and Martin

Luther King and has now become very popular in the New Age community. The fact that this method has been successfully used during the past hundred years to bring down despots and imperial tyranny is evidence that we are moving away from direct violence as a means for promoting peace, liberty and freedom.

The third is **Subordination** as a means of promoting transformation. Whereas insubordination means, simply not to do what is expected or asked of us, subordination means to work together or help. It is a conscious choice to co-operate with the enemy or the opposing force. This system was used by a Buddhist monk during the Mongol invasion of Tibet. It is said that on hearing of the forthcoming invasion, all the monks fled the monastery, except one monk who decided to stand still in the middle of the huge courtyard. The invading army was led by an infamous general on horseback. The general rode, followed by his men, up to the monastery, in through the gates, into the courtyard and up to the monk. The general drew his sword, pointed it towards the monk and said, *"Do you know who I am"*? The monk stood in silence, so the general said, *"I am the man who can thrust this sword through your heart without blinking"*. There was total silence around the courtyard, the monk asked, *"Do you know who I am"*? The general remained silent and so the monk said, *"I am the man who can let you thrust that sword through my heart without blinking"*.

This approach is based on the realisation that *"I have seen the enemy, it is us"*. To fight or be insubordinate towards another is to oppose oneself. In consciously co-operating with those who oppose us, we eliminate the enemy within and outside us.

Finally, I would like to introduce **The Way of Absence** whereby we become absent from any opposing forces or systems. We are simply not there, where we may find ourselves a threat to others or vice versa. Hence, stillness, silence, isolation and 'conscious suicide' are the means to bring about social peace and progress. For example, dolphins that are captured and kept in steel tanks die within three months, because they cannot escape , they commit suicide, simply by holding their breath until they die. The extreme example is self-immolation, which can be as powerful a tool for social reform as secret societies or massive movements.

I am proposing The Way of Absence as a means of social reform. We simply remove ourselves from the world of competition and coercion. If we do not acknowledge the struggle, in doing so we will not fuel the fire of force against force. Absence from resistance is a form of wisdom and when mastered, the world is yours. I can best explain its practice via a story:

A *man is sitting on a wall, waving a stick and laughing frantically. He is laughing because of the screams the passers by make as he strikes them with his stick. The secret of avoiding this collision of force would be to simply avoid the street altogether.*

Every time you encounter resistance, remember you are provoking it, albeit by being there. Resistance arises from the realm of illusion and subsides via the realm of reality. Hence your condition of *being* is the source of harmony – even in the midst of war.

185

Relating in Practice

As I sat quietly looking out across the horizon on a small beach in Cornwall, I felt myself being a part of the sky, sun, sea, clouds, wind and the Earth beneath my body. I cannot explain in words what I felt, as I felt everything there is to feel, in that moment. I have had this feeling many times since my childhood and with such completeness, that I have come to know how everything works together and becomes one.

All things become one by Relating.

This experience is the best example I can think of to demonstrate the practice of Relating. For me, Relating has been a mystical experience. I say mystical, because I have always been amazed at how so many diverse people and events enrich my life, as if by magic. The nature of Relating is miraculous: think of the crashing of the waves on the beach, birds singing, rainbows, and dowsing for water, all of which come from miraculous events of Relating. I feel that all I need to do for miracles to happen to me, is be open and willing to relate to nature, animals and people. When I talk about Relating, I mean the interplay of life with one's-*self*.

This is how it works. When you drink water, it becomes a part of your body. By relating with the air that you breathe, the food that you eat, sounds and smells, and the light and touch which enters your body, you become one. For example, when I touch you, the feeling enters your body and mind and becomes one with your being. In the same way, by relating to someone or something we become one. Since we are relating to our surroundings all the time, we should feel at one, but we don't. Why? Without The Pathway of Relating we feel separate and cannot become one with creation.

By Relating we witness the miracles of creation.

If you choose any event or item: the birth of a baby, a volcano, a flower, a grain of rice or a colour, behold, you are witnessing a miracle. A flower really is a miracle. Consider the odds against a tiny seed surviving, and the transcendent beauty it develops. Relating is our capacity to see, hear, touch, smell, taste, feel and appreciate what is happening in and around us. I asked at the beginning: what is the purpose of Relating? Why are we all relating right now in countless ways? To help what we are relating with. Relating to HELP, we create harmony, peace, prosperity, love, joy and so become one. The opposite of help is harm, creating disharmony, conflict, poverty, hate, suffering and separation. Relating to HELP, we can change disharmony to harmony, disunity to unity, poverty to prosperity and suffering to salvation, and if we are relating for the sole purpose of helping, all things will work for the common good.

The practice of Relating is to HELP, and it begins by helping oneself, through how we think and feel. This is what makes us help or harm others. Thinking helpful thoughts we feel harmony within, manifest helpful actions and create harmony in the world. If you are reading this book to help yourself or someone else, you are relating as a servant. In the same way, we have created the HELP book to help humanity, and we are your servants. The idea of 'servant-hood', is central to many spiritual traditions, but their practitioners often cannot serve one another.

Many people want to help each other but, without The Pathway of Relating, they remain separated and alienated. This breeds fear and leads to harm. The Pathway of Relating guides us to The Way of Relating and to the purpose of HELP. Relating to HELP enables us to fulfil all our individual and collective needs. Every act of help sends a harmonious vibration into the world, affecting all living things and the Earth.

The
Pathway
of

Creating

Reflections on Creating

My creativity is guided by my Being.

I enjoy my work for it is meaningful.

I receive fair pay for what I do for my employer.

I know how the creative process works and use it knowingly.

I create all the wealth I need and want.

I pay all my bills on time and with pleasure.

I create what I want by being true and honest.

I know how to turn fear into faith.

I know what it feels like to plant a tree, grow a vegetable or care for an animal.

I am a genius.

I am devoted to using my creative genius for the benefit of all.

My creativity reflects my spirituality.

When I encounter my own ego or that of others, I simply do not acknowledge it.

I encourage myself beyond all challenges.

I empower others to new heights of creativity and responsibility.

I complete my responsibilities on time or early.

I know how to handle the moments of isolation and exposure that I face as a pioneer in my field of creativity.

I know people who believe in me and what I want to create.

I realise that my creativity is a unique contribution to my community, humanity and the Earth.

As I grow, I feel myself becoming a spirit of creative enterprise.

The Role of Creating

A human being is capable of creating anything imaginable, but the idea of creating what we can imagine is not talked about in our conversations at home, schools or in society. What is paramount in the competitive culture we have created is work, and any work will do as long as it pays money. Work for most people is a means to an end, that means selling their bodies, skills and often their principles, in order to ensure their livelihood. The irony is that, 'the end', in this scenario is spiritual suicide and that is why Sunday is a sad day for many people. For many people Sunday has become a day of grief, because Monday means going back to work. For others, Sunday is worse because they are out of work and are on a downward spiral into the 'disposable class'. Working is the cause of a lot of suffering, in all cultures worldwide. If we are to create a life worth living, we must review what we call work. We begin by asking two questions.

What is work?

What is not work?

Although there are many ways to look at work, from a 'waste of time' to 'work as worship', it is the thing we call work, not money which drives our whole world culture. People often say, "money makes the world go around", as though we have no choice but to work for money. The problem is, most people, even the rich, work not because they need money, but because they have to in order to feel secure, worthy or powerful.

Security and success are the main motivation in today's capitalist, materialistic world culture, where the majority work against their will. The question is: if we have to work hard simply to survive and in order for a few to thrive, is this really a democracy? Is this the land of equal opportunity, liberty, and justice for all? Is this one nation

191

indivisible under God? If not, we must ask ourselves if work has become a subtle form of *slavery* and if so, *who* is making us work in this way and for what purpose? Do we work to nurture our needs or sustain the capitalist system? For generations we have been tricked into believing that money makes the world go around. It is *your* work and labour which moves your society, organisation and nation! Remember that the next time someone talks of making more money and ask them why?

What is work for?

We have to ask: where does the purpose for work come from, and why is there so much resistance to working in all cultures around the world? Our purpose in working has its roots in slavery, which was widespread in Egypt, Persia, Asia, Europe and America. Not so long ago, slavery was considered to be a natural and righteous way to use a lesser human being. Slaves worked for their masters and were bought and sold to the highest bidder. They did not work for money, but for food and to stay alive.

Slavery is the taking of a persons labour by law and force. We think slavery is something that happened long ago, but how many people around the world will have to work today simply to stay alive? When I was homeless, the way to get work was to stand on the street with a sign.

any work for food

When there was no work, I ate out of dustbins or went hungry. Today, millions of people are working for food, just as slaves worked for their masters. The difference now is that people cannot find work, even for food, which is worse than being a slave who is given food, shelter and clothing. Before the coming of slavery, human beings had the freedom to roam and forage for food, to find shelter and make clothes. Slavery denied the individual this freedom and now work denies human beings, not only the natural right to roam and forage, but also food and shelter, in the event of being without work. Were you brought up to believe that we work and live in a free society? Think again! You will find that people are controlled and exploited by the same institutions as those that prospered from slavery. These very same institutions are still in power today and as much a part of our social structure as they were a few thousand years ago. The time, energy, skills and labour of the best part of your life go into working for your employer. The question is: does working for an employer, rather than working with someone, have to mean a subtle form of slavery? Yes, because given the freedom, most workers would flee from their employers, just as slaves from their masters.

Fleeing from your employers, however, or overthrowing the capitalist system, is not going to set workers free. Fight and flight have been used for thousands of years and have not worked. Besides, who is going to leave their job, when without it there is no way to earn a living? People are terrified of losing their jobs, especially in countries without a welfare support system. The irony is: as the human population increases, work becomes scarce and unemployment rises. In many countries, because employers know there are no opportunities for work, they make people work harder, and lower wages to below sustenance level.

The question employers must ask is: what motivates me? Is my work driven by need and necessity or greed and glory? For the worker, liberation from slavery will come when they listen to the *call* of creativity. It is not through revolution that the workers of the world will unite and break their chains, but through evolving their work toward their creative calling. This transformation will take time to spread across the human population, but we need to start now. The first step toward working to be creative is for each worker to ask if they wish to be led by the call from one's self or from the system?

Who am I working for?
What am I working for?

Do you work to live or live to work? Are you working your life away in some purposeless and meaningless pursuit, given to you by your employer or by your own illusion? In The Pathway of Being, I said that there is a purpose in your life and there is a meaning beyond the everyday. This makes your calling not a *man made* venture, but a Divine one. The Franciscan monks believe that *"work is prayer"*, a spiritual contribution performed by physical action. Every person has been given a gift by God to help people. What is your gift and how can you help?

Our aim is to work and create the calling. By following your calling, you will separate yourself from the dread of man-made work. The Role of Creating is to enable you to create a way of being in the world, which is Divine.

The Way of Creating

Each one of us is a creative genius. The genius of creating begins in creation itself, and our journey of creating has been an epic adventure. It began in that flash of creation we call conception. We began by creating ourselves, by reaching the uterus and completing the task of being born into the strange and vast world outside the womb.

Life is a miracle. You are a miracle.
Creating miracles is your birthright.

Since our birth, the challenge has been to embrace all aspects of being human and create what we have come to complete. You are the result of the most creative act in the cosmos, the creation of life itself. That makes you the most powerful impulse in the whole of creation. Creating is your natural birthright, so what will you do with it?

Each one of us comes into the world to serve a purpose. We all have a personal purpose or gift. There is no such thing as a non-gifted person. The Pathway of Creating is a channel for expressing your uniqueness into the world. As unique individuals, we have the task of sharing our gift and completing what we were born to do. For example, I know that I was born to help and that by helping I express my gift of creativity. Just as a rose is a miracle, so every act of creating is a miracle. Look, you are witnessing a miracle in front of your eyes, right now by creating thought patterns which are completely unique.

A thought is a miracle creating other miracles.

Creating is manifested in walking, dancing, singing, speaking, and in all acts of creation. People use whatever they have for creating and expressing their natural gift. I am using words here to help people and in doing so I am sharing my gift of helping. What each of us is creating right now is our own gift to humanity and the Earth. When we look at it like this, what we create in every moment becomes the very pathway by which we go on creating.

Creating is not separate from living or a part time activity. It is a moment by moment process which is present in every thought, emotion and action. If Creating is a constant process of living, then what is work? Where does work come into the equation and what is its purpose? So many people work for eight or more hours in a day and still not have enough to provide food and shelter for their families. Work as we know it has become damaging to our lives because we have lost the link between work and life. But what is that link?

Living = Working = Creating

Here is how life works. Every cell in your body is working. Working is using energy for living. Living is working in order to create. Having a 'job', usually means doing someone else's work and promoting their life and creativity. Doing this means losing your birthright and your life being split between living and working. Working should be a response to our needs and our calling in life. Your work is often referred to as a 'calling'. Like your name, it calls you. It *is* you and the way you make a living.

Just like your name, a call is what we answer to. We have been trained to respond to whoever calls us, be they teachers, preachers, or employers, but are we what they call us? We are called by our names and the work that we do, but is that who we are? We have become what we have been called and now we respond to that call as if we had no choice. For example, when I am training teenagers on the L.I.Y.T. Programme*, I ask them, *"Who are you?"* and they tell me their names. Yes, you have a name, but that is not *who you are.* I tell them, "You are not what they call you, but the *calling* of what you have come to create." Once at the end of the seminar, a teacher

* Living Inspirations Youth Training Programme.

came and asked me if I would show her how to listen to her calling. I told the teacher, "listen to your-self and you will hear your calling". Your calling is *what you really need* and *what comes out*. Most people respond to the call of society like sheep running to the call of the shepherd. When you hear your call, wake up and work devotedly towards creating what it tells you.

What is my calling?

One's calling is intended to guide our gift toward creating the common good. The 'call' wakes us up, but we fall asleep again. We play it safe, make excuses or get discouraged. How do we follow our calling? We have all heard the call at least once in our lifetime, but what is it that prevents even the most powerful people from creating their calling? In my youth, I often wondered why the disciples and close friends of the spiritual leaders could not follow their footsteps?

To follow our calling we have to go into the unknown, which brings forth fear and doubt that often defeats the *will* to follow the call. For example, your calling can tell you to devote your life to helping children in need, but the fear of the unknown and the doubts about your capacity make you give second best or abandon the call. To justify abandoning the call, we look for excuses, find reasons and lay blame. Just as we abandon our calling, we ignore the call of the spiritual messengers.

To follow our calling we have to overcome *fear and doubt*, which hold us prisoners of our will. This sounds very inspiring, but how do we overcome all our fears, and doubts? For a lot of people, the suggestion of overcoming their fears and doubts seems impossible. That is why we abandon the call from the beginning or give up on the way. My aim is to show you the way to follow your calling as well as create the seemingly impossible. To demonstrate what I am saying I'd like to share my own calling. My calling is to help, which I heard at the age of sixteen. Since then, I have followed the call into the unknown and each step of this journey has been taken with what I call *The Sacred Steps.*

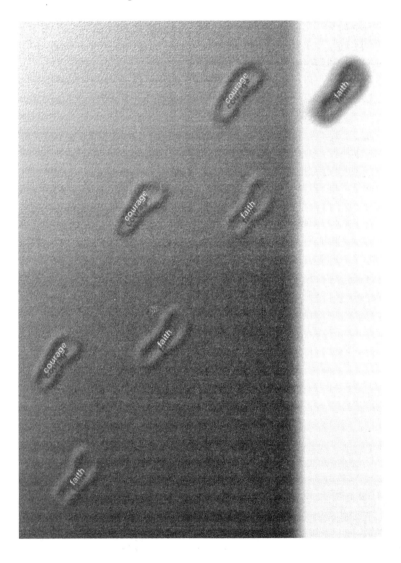

* The Sacred Steps taken from the Panlife teachings.

Going into the unknown in my teenage years was overwhelming and mastery of the unknown began with The Sacred Steps.

What are The Sacred Steps?

The Sacred Steps are the footsteps of the mind and body that will take you into the unknown. With these steps, I have overcome all fears and doubts to walk on the pathway of my calling. The Sacred Steps will enable you to overcome every fear and doubt on your journey of life. As you walk along The Pathway of Creating, your left foot represents courage and the right of faith.

Courage overcomes fear of the unknown and faith gives us hope to overcome the doubt of creating our calling. Courage and faith push us out of our cocooned existence into a new world, alive with new experiences. How creative would we all be if we walked The Sacred Steps anew and in all acts of creating? All acts of creation are powered by courage and faith, which we share with other human beings and all living things on the Earth.

Every living thing possesses the courage to create and the faith that life will support its development. If what I am saying is true, then courage and faith are inborn in every human being and every creature. This means that all were created by the creator with courage and faith, but the courage I speak of is not of the hero, and the faith is not of the scriptures. I mean natural, inherent courage and faith, which are sacred and inherent in all acts of creating.

The Sacred Steps awaken our natural courage and faith, the courage and faith we had when we first walked and believed we could create anything. A child has natural faith and courage, which you can see in its face and the way it behaves. Before we instill fear and doubt in our children, they really know intuitively that they are unlimited beings, living and creating works of pure genius. A child naturally believes that it is a genius, but what happens if I ask *you:*

Are you a genius?

The way you respond to this statement with your thoughts and feelings reveals what you believe you are capable of creating. You are the embodiment of the whole of creation, created by the creator, whose light shines through you. This means that you are capable of creating the calling which emanates from your being, and The Infinite Being. So, when I speak of genius, imagine the brilliance that emanates from anyone who puts their heart and soul into their calling. For me, genius is a personal trait between myself and my calling and not the genius recognised by others and paraded for the fanfare of society.

Even though we may never paint a picture, write a book, compose a musical masterpiece or create a new invention, we all have the capacity to commit ourselves to our calling and become a genius, creating masterpieces out of every action, no matter how ordinary they may be. In this sense, each one of us is a genius, capable of creating the seemingly impossible in any work undertaken, but if we are all geniuses, why isn't the world abundant with the *handiwork of geniuses*? Where have we lost the genius of being human?

One reason for the lack of brilliance in our society, is the denial of the individual's birthright of creative expression. From birth, our earliest actions are brimming with creative energy, our young children create in alignment with their calling and therefore portray that unique genius. Look at the drawing style copied by Picasso or recall a common saying, "Wisdom comes from the mouth of babes". The infant bloom of genius is soon crushed or educated out of us. Individual expression is replaced by conformity and learning to copy and please, rather than create and originate.

To deny one's creativity is to ignore one's calling. People have abandoned their calling in favour of material consumerism. The incessant consuming of materials has led us to bury our own creativity under a mountain of *things*. The media and our modern education systems conspire to trick people, especially the young, into focusing on consumerism and careers rather than creating their calling. Although our homes are full of material possessions, our hearts are often empty, and our souls abandoned.

Human beings, the most creative creatures on the Earth, have created a world of mass production, mass marketing, mass transportation, mass media, and mass education. We live in a *mass* culture where very often everyone looks, smells, dresses and even behaves identically. Conformity, not creativity, has become the main *order* in our educational and social institutions. Creativity is not considered a natural condition of being human, but more a quirk or privilege reserved for a few eccentrics. That is why society lacks creative geniuses.

Our aim must be to return to our calling and express the genius of the gift that is our birthright. We begin by listening to our own calling and then following The Pathway of Creating. As you walk along your Pathway of Creating, a voice will come up in you with your calling. Put your heart and soul into creating your calling and the genius within you will shine brilliantly.

Genius is born of Creating.

Creating anything for the first time, from baking a loaf of bread to flying to Mars, means going into the unknown. Creating something new is the most challenging activity, for it makes profound and extreme demands on the creator. It takes us into new states and spaces of the human experience.

In these moments of doubt and uncertainty, we need some sure way of overcoming the extreme challenges which often cause many to fall by the wayside. History is littered with men and women who had extraordinary visions and yet did not manage to come remotely close to completing their life's mission. Is there a wish or any work that you have the yearning to manifest?

Everyone has at least one idea or wish in their lifetime which they wish they could make come true. Wishing by itself will not make it happen! Millions of people have wild and wonderful ideas, but these are forgotten or shelved because of the lack of creative know-how. People who do not know how to realise their dreams tend to build them up in their heads or bury them in order to make life bearable. Those who do embark on daring adventures often waste their efforts by making unnecessary mistakes. When you make a mistake or bodge up a project, where does it come from? It is often a result of not knowing The Way of Creating! In the same way, creating a fulfilling career, relationship, home or family life all begins and ends in the creative process.

The Way to Creating anything is contained in four fundamental stages: *Clarity, Perseverance, Endurance* and *Completion*. In knowing how to use these stages consciously, we minimise making mistakes and increase the chances of completing what we set out to do. We should start by practising them on little projects and then proceed on to greater things.

Clarity is the first step in our creative adventure. Why? If you don't know where you are going, you will end up somewhere else. Unclear perception is like living in a box, seeing life through a pin hole. Many famous, respected and influential people are only better off than the masses because their pin hole is bigger. Often we work for schemes and dreams which the mind sees through the pinhole.

We have to dismantle the box we live in, but how do we do that? By separating illusion from reality, (see pages 110–119). Although you can use many techniques to clear the mind, if you can't see with clarity where illusion is divided from reality, your mind will become caught in illusions again. The worst aspect of this is that you get preoccupied with constantly clearing the mind. This restricts creativity. Many spiritual people spend a lot of time praying and meditating, trying to keep the mind clear. Dismantle your box of illusion and your creativity will flow with the force of God.

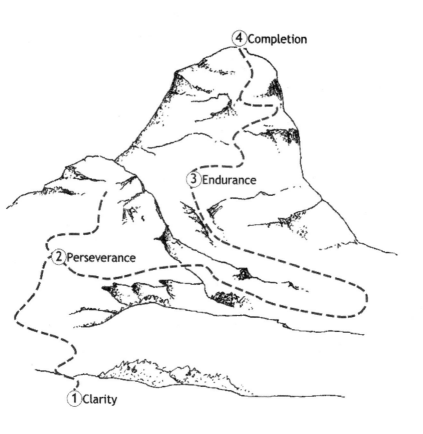

Pan Pathways: The four Stages of Creating

Every act of Creating is guided by four Stages of Creating. In knowing The Way of Creating, your chances of completion will not be left to chance. The Pathway of Creating will guide you from the call-to-completion. The more you study and practice these stages, the more creatively fulfilled you will be.

Once your mind is clear, you will hear the call of God. Your calling is the driving force behind your creativity. When your mind is clear, the calling of God can be heard constantly. When this happens, you are out of the box and into the world of boundless creativity. If on the way, your life becomes 'closed in', remember the 'flies in the bottle analogy'*. All you have to do is turn your back on the realm of illusion and fly towards the realm of reality.

Close your eyes and use your imagination to shift your perception and direction towards a clear aim. The lack of imagination is that we find change difficult, since we can see or imagine reality being different from that which it is now. Unless you can clearly imagine your goal, how do you know which way to go, or even when you have arrived? When your mind is clear, imagine what you want to create. If you can clearly imagine your aim, it will happen. Once you have formed a clear image in your mind, devote your life towards its creation. Start! The best way to embark on giant projects is to start. There comes a time when all the praying, planning and preparation is done. Then we must have the courage to take a leap of faith – ACT. The way to 'move mountains', is to think big, and act *now*. Faith comes with a shovel!

Perseverance is the second stage, which involves finding the ways and means to go forward and overcome unforeseen challenges. No matter how carefully you plan your journey of creativity, there are always new obstacles and opportunities to deal with. In the dictionary, perseverance means *steadfast pursuance of an aim* and, in theological terms, *continuance in a state of grace*. Perseverance without the grace of God is a senseless pursuit of illusions. Is it any wonder that most people give up at this stage or start taking short cuts and sacrifice their principles.

When this happens, you have reached a point where you have to step out in faith. When you have faith to step beyond your limits, God will bless you with everything you need and more. In my journey of creativity, there have been many times when the grace of God has

*See page 141.

helped me persevere. For example, when God asked me to create the HELP book and disseminate it worldwide, I knew nothing about writing or publishing. Since then every mistake, obstacle and challenge has been overcome through perseverance.

The bible says, *"When one door closes, another door opens."* Never think of a situation as hopeless. If you do, then it will become so. Instead, have faith and persevere. Nothing worthwhile is achieved without faith and nothing extraordinary is created without extraordinary faith. For example, it took Ian Fleming thirty years to get Penicillin accepted in mainstream medicine *after* he had discovered its medical benefits. Another brilliant demonstration of perseverance was by an uneducated man named Thomas Edison, who invented the light bulb after eight thousand experiments.

Perseverance is a demonstration of faith.

With God on your side nothing is impossible. The more faith you have, the more you can persevere against all odds, limitations and obstacles. When I was a boy, my mother used to tell me the story of Noah. To me, Noah represents the perfect demonstration of perseverance – faith. To think that an *ordinary* man could devote forty years of his life creating a vision that no one else believed in.

When you can persevere through all challenges, your faith will become perfect and nothing or no one will make you falter. Adversity and every 'hopeless' situation will be a golden opportunity to prosper, by the grace of God. That is why, every time there is a set back in The HELP Programme, it has been followed in the coming days, weeks and years, with miraculous increase. The same will be demonstrated with the publication of this book.

Endurance is the third stage and perhaps the most demanding, for this is the furthest point you have been so far on your journey of creativity. Having their first child is an experience of endurance all mothers are familiar with. Nothing can prepare you for the unknown areas of childbirth and the extreme demands it will make. The same applies to all creative adventures where the individual has to pioneer. In any field of creativity, pioneers need to endure the moments of exposure to the unknown. The unknown is a forbidding place, where very few venture.

Endurance is a demonstration of will.

As you enter the unknown all kinds of doubts, uncertainties, insights, truth and beauty may take you into strange and altered states of being. The secret is to hang on until they pass. Endurance means, 'to keep going', moving on from where you are. Endurance develops maturity and character, which comes from the courage and the will to go the distance. Do what you will to lift yourself and let go of *everything* which is unnecessary or the dead weight will weigh you down.

There are many people who start the journey, yet only a few make it past the post of endurance. The others are either not ready or do not believe they can complete the journey. The final part of endurance is what I call *being there*, which is composed of a moment to moment sequence of events which are beyond time and space. Endurance takes us out of the comfort zone and beyond every limitation, making us experience the limitless nature of our being.

Most spiritual people want an easy journey. They say, "I will try," not, "I will do." If you are about to quit, then endure and believe that you will complete. Leave the past behind you and burn your bridges as you go forward. When you find yourself flagging in your faith be still and count your blessings. As you count your blessings, your faith will increase.

The endurance stage can last for days or decades, depending on the nature of your journey. Once you have found a way to reach your goal, you become focused on one thing – completion. During the endurance stage, the creator often runs out of steam. The power to continue the journey from here on in, comes from *the will*. Willpower propels us in the final moments, days or decades of endurance, into the final stage of completion.

When you feel the agony of endurance, have the courage and faith to continue. At this point we want somebody to help us, but there are some things you have to go through yourself. If you have a few faithless days, don't worry. All is not lost. Pray and return to faith. Faith is like a cow. You can lose many pails of milk, but do not lose the cow.

Those of you who are in the endurance stage in your journey will know what I am saying. You feel stretched beyond your limits, to such a point that you hear yourself scream. Do not worry, as God is with you. As you feel alone and isolated, look behind you and you will see footsteps. They are not yours, but God's, who has been carrying you. Rise to the challenge. Rest if you need to, but keep your eyes on the goal.

Many people become disillusioned at this stage, because they set out with illusory goals which they cannot believe in, when push comes to shove. If you want to have the power-help of God, to complete your journey, then make sure you set out with the goal that God gives you.

Completion is the fourth and final stage. To *complete* means *to finish, make whole* and in secular terms, *to reach perfection, have everything, hold no more, overflow.* In a kind of coup de grace it can even mean, *to crown* but my favourite meaning of it is *to enjoy.* When we complete an action or bring a vision to completion, we feel full of joy. Even the completion of the smallest action does this. Completion appears very easy and it is. If we could complete, our lives would be overflowing with joy. Every time we complete, we feel joy and the more we complete, the more joy we feel and it overflows.

The truth is, very few people complete each experience, let alone their life's work. No sooner have we started one action, than we run to the next, hoping that's where it's at. Why do we do this? There are two main reasons: fear and the lack of help. Why fear? Because in completing every experience, we will become more comfortable and fulfilled in every aspect of our lives – an abundance of joy. Most of us are capable of handling all kinds of adversity and are familiar with suffering, but when it comes to being *totally* comfortable… That is the unknown which triggers fear. So, we sabotage the final stage of completion to remain in the known.

HELP is perhaps the most important part of the journey, for no matter how capable and independent we may be, no one can complete impossible challenges all by themselves. Even the thought of someone being with us in person, or in spirit encourages us to persevere, endure and complete projects which are otherwise beyond our reach. The story of Noah is the perfect example of *clarity, perseverance, endurance and completion*, made possible by the help of God. Even Jesus said, *"God help me,"* on the cross and with God's help he completed his mission.

Many people achieve remarkable results in business, education, politics, sport, art, music and so on. How many of these are man-motivated ventures – illusory? How much of the hype we see in the media about man's extraordinary achievements are delusions of grandeur, born of illusions?

Without God's help, humans are limited in what they can create. God makes you into unlimited beings. If you try to do it all yourself, you will burn out, give up or complete what *you* can. I often hear people say, *"I can't do everything myself"*. But you can do everything God wants you to do. With God's help, imagine what you can complete.

Nearing completion brings us full circle. We need to recall that clarity and motivation which has brought us on this journey, from the starting point on the map where we perceived our destination. Then you believed it was possible. Now at the completion, you need the touchstone of faith once more. Thank God.

Bills

Bills! Why, you may ask do I bring up the topic of bills in The Pathway of Creating? Well, the way we pay our bills determines what we create with our lives. Although bills or payment is one of the major preoccupations in our lives, we very rarely discuss it. The issue of bills or payment, be it for services, taxes, borrowings, employment, rent etc., almost always brings anxiety to peoples' faces. Watch the reaction of your family or colleagues when they are face to face with a bill. Why does the thought of payment evoke such anxiety, grief and fear in us? Bills have such a grip on our minds and have become so much a part of our lives that we are not aware of how much we are affected by them.

If you look closely, you will see how many of your ideas, choices, emotions and actions are influenced by how much things cost. For example, are you stuck in your job, relationship, where you live and what you eat, because of your worry of not being able to afford the change? What is your attitude towards bills?

Things could be worse, you may say, but how long can you go on paying before you are simply existing to pay bills? Given the choice, would you opt out of paying bills? Would you prefer to live in a world where there is no money or payment of any form? If we went back to hunting and gathering, bartering or another system of exchange, would that free us from the bondage of payment? I think not, since there is a law of give and take which we cannot escape. We could change the means of exchanging goods and services, but the fears and phobias will still remain, until we change our attitudes to giving and receiving. A person who cannot give and receive freely is far more paranoid about payment than one who is not.

Payment is simply an act of giving.

It is not the amount that determines one's response to payment, but our attitude towards payment in general. Most people see payment as a burden and pay for what they receive begrudgingly, even for things they need. How many times do we hear parents say, *"Do you know how much it costs to feed, clothe and school you"*? When we view anything as a burden, it becomes a burden and ultimately cripples us. Do you feel burdened by your bills?

Our aim is to pay with pleasure. Since we have to pay for what we receive sooner or later and whether we like it or not, we may as well pay with thanks. In which way do you view payment for the goods and services you receive, as a punishment or a privilege? Since we have to pay for everything, your answer will illustrate how miserable or pleasurable your life is.

Whether you are rich or poor, look forward to paying your bills and think how much you will enjoy the smallest things. When you take your friends out for a meal, do you remember the bill or the meal? When you can take pleasure in paying, then what you are paying for becomes pleasurable. If you view payment as a punishment, then every payment will be felt as punishment.

When we start paying with pleasure, we affirm limitless wealth and abundance. A person who hates payment will attract lack and limitation. People who are always talking lack and limitation reap lack and limitations. I have heard many a 'wise man and woman' talk about creating a better world and yet cannot pay for what they want to create. Have you ever wondered why spiritual organisations and charities never have enough money to pay for their projects? Surely a truly spiritual person or organisation can create as much money or wealth as they need?

Can you imagine yourself being able to pay for creating your calling? If you can't, then you are still stuck and poor. If you can, then you are rich and free to create anything imaginable. How does it work? Payment in any form is a force which moves spirally and comes back to its creator. How you pay for what you receive today will determine whether you are heading for a life of lack or abundance. Remember this, even the wealthiest people can live in lack for fear of not having enough.

When people do not have enough money, they beg, steal, borrow, gamble or work harder, and still they never have enough. Why? The way to have an abundance of money is to release it. How do you *release* money? Let me ask you, do you spend your money like it's your own? Yes? From now on spend money as though it belongs to God and you will spend it wisely, freely and joyfully.

I know that the way to become free from debt and poverty is by paying and giving joyfully. To demonstrate, let me tell you that I have no debts, not even a mortgage, nor do I owe money to anyone. I have become prosperous simply by paying and giving whatever I have with joy. For me, payment is the planting of seeds which grow, bear fruit and multiply. From *one* payment there comes back love, money, materials, resources and services, multiplied manyfold.

A handful of coins.

There was a time when all I had was a handful of coins, and the vision of creating a worldwide programme was overwhelming. Then came the knowing: with a handful of seeds you can grow an orchard. By using that handful of coins according to the will of God, every provision has been given to fulfil the vision.

Look how The HELP Programme continues to grow like an unexplained phenomenon. That handful of coins entered the mainstream of money and keeps coming back multiplied. So the increase of prosperity goes on providing us with all the money we need to help humanity.

Procreative Living

The discovery of Human Evolution and Life Procreation, has revealed a completely new way of managing our lives. What is procreative living? A way of being creative in accordance with The Infinite Being. But, why do we need to learn how to live procreatively if we are already believers? Procreative living is a means of management which enables you to take full responsibility of yourself and our society, to declare the work of God.

Many spiritual people believe in God, but cannot marry their belief in business, management, organisation and government. The result is not only hypocrisy by way of a dual existence, but also the lack of competence to *manifest* the work of God. Have you ever asked yourself why you or your peers or the most spiritual leaders in your faith have not assumed authority for your nation? By authority I mean the wisdom of stewardship to fulfil the responsibility of helping people. Who else but the Godly are the best qualified to manage the power and resources of your nation? If God is with you, why are the Godless in authority over you and governing your nation?

Before I explain Procreative Living, let us look at the current methods of living and managing our existence.

Reactive people are often controlled by their physical environment. Reactive people are driven by their instincts. They react impulsively to external stimulus, be it on television, at work or on the street. If the weather is good they feel good, if the weather is bad then their attitude and performance goes down.

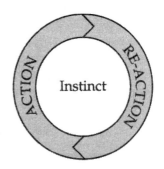

Proactive people carry their own weather with them. Whether it rains or shines makes no difference to them. The essence of a procreative person is the ability to use any adverse situation or advantage as an opportunity for growth and prosperity. Proactive people follow their intelligence, not their instincts. They have the initiative and the responsibility to make things happen. This is why a lot of powerful, rich people are proactive. However, being proactive does not necessarily mean a healthy state to be in. Hitler and his commanders were very proactive.

Proactivity is often ego driven and can result in domination. It lacks the intuitive impulse which originates from Infinite Being. Turn on the news and you will see how many of our leaders in the church, state and government are proactive. They are preoccupied with the duality of profit and power, success and greatness; their ego is in control.

Procreative people are driven by intuition. Procreative people live four-dimensionally. They are intuitively guided and use their proactive freedom to do the Will of the *infinite spirit.* They are motivated by service which brings goodness, not greed and greatness. A truly procreative person can make things happen without position or possession, because they are propelled by the infinite force-God. Procreative living is a new dimension of existence in human evolution. How do we actually move from a reactive, to proactive, to a procreative way of living?

The transformation from reactive to proactive to procreative is done by changing our thoughts and beliefs.

The first stage is to replace fear with faith. It is the fear of 'lack' and 'not enough' which prevents us from living procreatively. You have to understand that the Earth has sustained all living things on its surface since the dawn of creation. It is the only planet in our solar system that sustains and supports life: from the air we breathe, the sun which keeps us warm, the fruits of the trees to the water in the seas. The whole ecosystem of this planet is solely oriented towards sustaining and promoting Human Evolution and Life Procreation. Just as the Earth is procreative by nature, so are *you*.

The second stage is to start using intuition. *The key to procreative living.* Living by intuition is understanding and acknowledging that the Earth is *on our side*. This is why new born animals naturally feel the Earth is a safe place to *be*. Instead of trying to control nature and your life with reasoning and intellect, let intuition guide you. At first you may occasionally have flashes of illumination or intuition, then fall back into the world of darkness. Be patient, be still and be poised to pick up your intuitive leads. Be ready to enter what Jesus called 'The Kingdom'.

The third stage is choice. Everyday, we have the opportunity to totally transform the quality of our existence. Today, you will have at least seventy thousand choices and yet over ninety five percent of your behaviour may be the same as yesterday. Life is not a chance, it's a choice. You can make one choice today and forever change the way you live. If you choose to have miracles happen to you, so they shall. Expect miracles in your health, home, family and creativity. Your subconscious mind will then manifest miracles. Maybe you need a financial miracle! Choice: the metaphysical law of attraction will activate the physical law of supply and demand. Faith, intuition and choice will bring you new life.

Creativity and Responsibility

Creativity and responsibility are two sides of the same coin. When you hear the call of creativity, it will be followed by the responsibility to make it happen. When you hear the call of hunger, who takes the responsibility to feed you? You do! In the same way, every call of creativity carries with it the responsibility of its fulfilment. Creativity without responsibility leaves us powerless and unable to respond to our calling. Responsibility without creativity results in a lifeless pursuit of activities which lack spiritual substance or satisfaction.

What is your Creativity?
What is your Responsibility?

Whether we know it or not, each one of us has come into the world to perform our function. In fact every thought and action is another step towards completing what we have come to do. This journey, from conception to death, is referred to as one's destiny. The notion of destiny is often misunderstood and shrouded in mystery. For me, destiny has two sides, personal and universal – the personal destiny of my own life and the universal destiny of humanity and the whole.

At the moment of conception we enter into a body which then assumes our identity. Then we give this identity a name. Your name becomes your truth. Personal destiny is based on personal truth – what we believe to be true for ourselves. For example, a child believes its ball belongs to it and to no-one else. In the same way, we are brought up to believe that all our possessions, including the body, belong to us. This is our personal truth and we have the responsibility to take care of what has been entrusted to us.

We take care of ourselves by eating, learning, working, buying a house, having a family etc. In order to fulfil our personal destiny, we must focus on taking responsibility for our own needs and wants. Fulfilling personal responsibility comes from our instinctual nature and can be traced back millions of years. All animals spend the majority of their time and energy performing actions which ensure their survival. Because our survival is the most important thing, we too tend to focus on 'me' and 'what is mine'. Unlike animals, human beings have the capacity to comprehend a bigger picture in which they can consciously participate.

The ability to contribute consciously to the whole is the ability to fulfil one's universal responsibility. Of course, all of this sounds very nice in words, but what does it actually mean to embark on a journey to fulfil one's universal destiny? Although the notion of universal responsibility sounds enormous, even impossible, it is in truth very simple and easy. The question is, how can universal responsibility be as easy as taking care of ourselves? With individual responsibility, we follow our instincts; with universal responsibility, we follow our intuition. We surrender our will selflessly to do what is necessary for the whole. The Bible says, *"Do not as I will, but as thou wilt."* Life gets easier the further we evolve from the animals and the more responsibility we can fulfil.

The two main reasons why we do not embark on fulfilling our universal responsibility is that we think we are alone and therefore powerless. The following analogy may help to change that. Imagine yourself as part of the ocean. One day you come ashore and, like a salt doll, you wander far and wide. You feel lonely and lost. Returning to the same place, you enter the ocean again and once more become part of the whole. Intuition reconnects us to the whole. The way to put this analogy into practice is contained in the following words:

Infinite spirit guide me to do your will.

Listening to our intuition is the first step towards assuming universal responsibility. The second is to act in accordance with the guidance. We often talk about being unlimited beings, but what is it that stops us from demonstrating those words or wishes? *Fear.*

There comes a time when all the thinking, all the meditating, praying and preparation has been done. The one thing that is left is the actual leap into the unknown, somewhat like a chick leaving the nest on its first flight. That leap is powered by the invisible force of *Faith.* How do you take that leap?

How can you fulfil your universal responsibility?

With your words and your work. What does that mean? When God reveals your calling, voice it with your words and work devotedly to fulfil it. By your words you activate your faith; by your works you fulfil your responsibility. With your words and your work you can create or destroy.

Look closely at what you have created or destroyed and you will come to understand the power of your words and work. Take a few moments to reflect on the words and work Jesus performed to fulfil his responsibility. By the age of thirty-three he fulfilled his universal responsibility without possession or position. Is there a limit to how much responsibility you can fulfil?

When I heard my calling to help humanity, I proclaimed the work of God with my words. Every word activates my faith and every action works toward fulfilling my responsibility. Look how my words and work are spreading HELP across the Earth. The Bible says *'God created everything we see with faith filled words'.* Only with your words and your work will you fulfil your God-given responsibility.

Creating in Practice

Every creature on the Earth is working towards creating comfortable conditions of living, now and for the future. For example, the amoeba, one of the smallest creatures on our planet, is creating its own life sustaining conditions. Although the amoeba is without sight, hearing, taste, smell or a brain, it is constantly creating a more comfortable situation. Living comfortably is the first call of Creating.

What am I Creating?

Unlike the amoeba, human beings have senses and a brain, but why are we not creating more comfortable conditions for living? Despite our creative capacity, we have been misguided into creating conditions which are harmful to our existence. Humans are the only creatures who are using their creative potential to destroy the very planet that sustains them. The purpose of Creating is to learn how to create *new* and *better* conditions of living. The way we are living shows what we have created and are creating for the future.

The true measure of my creativity is not assessed by what I have produced, amassed, invented or built, but what I have created of *myself.* I am the measure of my creativity and it is *who I am* that portrays what I have created. A musician, for example, creates a beautiful melody. Who is the genius? The creator! In the same way, we have to understand that we are the essence of our creativity and every act of creating is to nurture and create oneself. When this happens, living becomes Creating and every idea, emotion, thought and action works towards creating our calling.

Simple as it may be, the practice of creating begins with nurturing oneself. You are the person who has been called and by nurturing yourself, you nurture your calling. This is somewhat like a tree which nurtures itself in order to grow and bear fruit. We need to nurture ourselves to grow and fulfil the responsibility of our calling. Creating our calling begins with the call to fulfil our primal needs and, by nurturing ourselves, we have the power to project our calling into the world.

To nurture is to create.

A common folly of individuals who are devoted to their calling is that they neglect or sacrifice the basic needs of being human. Creating your calling is very demanding and the lack of self-nurture will hinder you from completing the mission, in profound ways. For example, Jesus had a calling. He said, *"I have come to establish the Kingdom of Heaven on Earth,"* but the scriptures tell us that, *"Foxes have holes, birds have nests, but the son of man had nowhere to lay his head."* What was the knock-on effect of being without a home, family and work, on the life of Jesus? In what way did this condition affect his decisions, levels of patience and the outcome?

Ironically, our Home, Health, Family and Work determine the condition of our whole existence. Each one of us, in our own way, is trying to create a more comfortable existence, but so many suffer from the poor condition of these foundations. To use an extreme example, every thirty-five seconds, another person commits suicide. Why? The condition of these foundations have a profound effect on the human being. By focusing our creativity on these foundations, we begin to create a personal 'Heaven on Earth'. I believe that Home, Health, Family and Work are the foundations for its creation – for the creation of our future.

What kind of a future world do you want to create?

I ask you, because the future of humanity and the Earth is being formed by what you and I are creating in every moment. Every act of creation affects our future. When we look at creating in this way, we become aware of the potential to create the future and what effects our actions are having in and around the world. The Way of Creating holds mythical powers to create worlds far beyond our imagination. When I am training candidates at The PAN Academy, I often begin by telling them that they are the most powerful person in the world. You are capable of Creating anything imaginable.

Many people are simply not aware of their awesome potential and often lack the support to project their calling on communal, regional, national and global levels. Imagine what you could create if you had all the help you needed. The practice of Creating begins with The Way of Being, then Knowing, Relating and Creating our calling. Our aim is to project our God-given calling into the world. The four Pathways of Being, Knowing, Relating, and Creating have helped me to project my calling and will enable you to move forward towards your own. Each one of us has our own unique purpose, and by working towards our calling, we *merge together* in the creation of our future.

The future is born of Creating.

Pathways
to

Paradise

Pan Paradise

Paradise! I always leave this topic until the end of my talks, in the hope that people have by now become more open to the possibility of creating a Pan Paradise* on Earth. Pan means *one complete whole* and the word Paradise is symbolic of the *Garden of Eden* or *Heaven on Earth*. What does the notion of Paradise or Heaven evoke in your imagination? Do you feel inspired, sceptical, misled, doubtful, cynical, hopeful?

Do you believe that you can live in a condition of Paradise? Even the most spiritual people do not believe that they can live in a paradise now. Every religion has been ordained to create Paradise or Heaven on Earth however, many of our leaders in church and state do not even declare it a possibility, let alone live in Paradise. Why? Because they lack *the way* to create a living Paradise.

Jesus said, *"I have come to build the Kingdom of Heaven on Earth."* Yet the church of Christ has neither preached nor presented even a blueprint to get us started. Why? Many people dare not speak of building paradise for fear of ridicule and rejection. Have you ever heard a sermon on 'the way to create paradise in your own life'? Is it surprising that many people find it easier to picture war, destruction, doomsday and Armageddon! I believe it is the divine right of every human being to live in paradise. That is why, deep down, we yearn to live in what we imagine it to be.

What is your picture of Heaven?
What is your picture of Paradise?

What is Paradise? Is it possible to create a paradise which is both personal and planetary? If it is possible, how can we get billions of people from different races, religions and nations to co-operate in the creation of Pan Paradise on Earth? These central

* Pan Paradise taken from the Panlife teachings.

222

questions are overwhelming. They induce doubt and separate people from the goal of creating Paradise on Earth. There is, however, a universal and practical way to paradise which will unite and mobilise people around the world. It is this, the means to create Pan Paradise on Earth, that I am going to present to you. By Paradise I do not mean a state of bliss brought forth by religious rituals, transcendental techniques, hallucinogenic substances or by amassing wealth and power. A person living in a condition of paradise is not always blissful, but in a state of being at peace and ease in the world, in the here and now. Many religious people aspire to live in paradise in the after life, but live in physical and spiritual suffering in this life. Open your mind to a new way of looking at paradise for here is the way to *actually* create a living paradise.

I want you to imagine *your* own ideal vision, your own dream or definition of paradise. Whatever that may be, does it have the wish for peace and ease? Why do I ask? Well, the wish for peace and ease is inherent in all life. Take the smallest life form on the Earth, the amoeba. It is without limbs, senses or a brain and yet it always chooses to move to a more comfortable situation. The need to be comfortable is driven by the wish for peace and ease.

If what I am saying is true, then peace and ease are universal preconditions to paradise. Therefore, until we create peace and ease in our own lives, we shall not live in paradise. My equation for paradise is very simple.

Peace + Ease = Paradise

Is my explanation of the nature of paradise *too simple, too easy or too true?* Could the nature of paradise really be as straightforward as experiencing peace and ease in every moment of your life? The more at peace and ease you are, the more your life will become comfortable, until you will experience paradise.

Now, let me explain what I mean by peace and ease. Being at peace and ease brings harmony and balance to our whole being. Peace brings forth spiritual well-being, and ease, physical well-being. Paradise resides at the point of balance where there is harmony between the physical and spiritual aspects of your life. For there to be peace and ease, there must be balance between the physical (body) and spiritual (mind). Paradise is where physical and spiritual needs are fully met.

I have seen those who have peace of mind, but lack ease in their body. Others have ease in their body but lack peace of mind. Peace without ease is like a forest without trees. One cannot exist without the other. Yes, you can use self-denial, mind control techniques or substances to remain unattached to the needs of the body and mind, but they will always deny you peace and ease.

The nature of paradise is like a seesaw. You have to nurture and balance the physical and spiritual equally. Look at your physical and spiritual condition. Do you feel at peace and ease? Ask yourself whether you spend as much time on the physical (material) as you do on the metaphysical (spiritual).

What is Peace?

Imagine yourself standing on the bank of a deep lake on a stormy day. Everything around you is being blown in random directions, the wind, waves, rain, leaves and the birds. This is the changing nature of the world. As you enter the lake and dive deeper and deeper, it becomes more and more still. On the surface there is chaos and below there is total stillness, calm. In the same way, the deeper you go within yourself, the calmer and more peaceful you will become. A peaceful person is one who is living at the centre of their being and therefore remaining at peace regardless of all conditions and actions. By peaceful I do not mean to be 'cool' or 'controlled'. A truly peaceful person has made peace with the world and become harmless.

What is Ease?

Imagine that you have everything you need to live comfortably right now. You have air to breath, water to drink, food to eat, clothes to keep you warm, shelter and a bed to rest your body. You have friends and family, money and prosperity, work that you enjoy and perfect health. In addition, you have faith and the promise of a long and prosperous future. If you had all these things would you feel at ease? Real ease is when all our natural needs are met.

In the same way, if you did not have what you needed or denied yourself these things, would you feel at ease? Are *you* at ease? Do you know anyone who is at ease constantly? Why are so many people from all walks of life living in a condition of dis-ease? Is there not enough? Do we not care for ourselves? How can we bring real and lasting peace and ease into our lives? Every living being wants to live in peace and ease, wants paradise. What we need is a simple and practical way to create a living paradise for ourselves, humanity and the Earth.

The Way to Paradise

The Way of HELP is the way to live life in paradise – as you are meant to. Our aim is to live in Pan Paradise and nothing less will do! To actually live in paradise may seem so far removed from your present condition, that I ask you to bear with me while I explain the way to move towards paradise.

The wish to create paradise is not new. The idea of it is born in every human being and it is promised by every religion. Just as an acorn contains the secret of the forest, each one of us knows the 'idea of paradise'. It is a very ancient and universal notion, but is it possible? Yes. Jesus said, *"I have come to build the Kingdom of Heaven on Earth,"* and that makes Heaven or Paradise on Earth a God-given goal. Jesus also said, *"What is impossible for man is possible for God."*

All of God's work through every person, prophet, messenger and the messiah has been aimed at the creation of Paradise on Earth. If paradise is our God-given goal, what has prevented us from reaching that goal? Why are so many 'living in hell' on Earth? So far, the creation of paradise has meant offering penance, wading through sacred texts, prolonged periods in meditation, renunciation and even self-flagellation. Are these really the way to paradise?

What is The Way to Paradise?

The idea of paradise is ancient but has it become an *ideal* because we do not know how to create it? Has this inevitably led to disbelief and vice versa? The Bible says, *"Everything the Kingdom can afford is yours"*. But how many people do you know who can say, 'My life is paradise'? Are you *still* waiting for a messiah to come and build the Kingdom of Heaven for you? The time has come to start building Pan Paradise on Earth. So where do we start? What are the *building blocks* for *"the Kingdom of*

Heaven on Earth"? What is the *process* by which we can create it?

The Way of HELP is the way to Pan Paradise. We start to create Pan Paradise on Earth by helping ourselves, and by living in peace and ease. The world starts with myself. My life is paradise and if you become a person who works and rests in peace and ease, then your life will also become paradise. Do you have a lot of trouble and strife in your life? Well, trouble comes from a lack of peace and strife robs you of ease. Paradise comes from peace and ease.

My paradise comes from living in a condition of complete and constant peace and ease, both of which can be created by simply focusing on The Foundations of HELP: Health, Home, Family and Work. A lot of people meditate and pray for peace and ease, but their Health, Home, Family and Work are in poor condition. Of course you can attain bliss by meditating and praying, but the moment you stop, your life will return to trouble and strife. That is why billions of believers who meditate and pray everyday, live in trouble and strife!

Your Health, Home, Family and Work are your *source* of peace and ease, but if you neglect them , there will be trouble and strife in your life. If you have created trouble and strife, you can create paradise. The way to create *real* and *lasting* peace and ease is by nurturing the foundations of your life. Many people want world peace, but do not have peace in their own lives. World peace will not come from campaigns, charities, religions, treaties, Nobel prizes, and conferences, but from *you*. By nurturing our foundations of living daily, we heal our dis-ease into ease. Ease is the pre-condition to peace and together they create paradise.

Health, Home, Family and Work
are The Foundations of Pan Paradise.

At first glance, these foundations of living appear too simple or basic to be of any significant importance to human evolution.

That is a predictable response in a world where very basic needs are overlooked. When I was living on the street, I would often go into churches, temples, synagogues and monasteries seeking guidance. I was told to pray, meditate, chant, serve, fast and so on. These practices made me feel good for a while, but did not serve my deep rooted needs, in fact, they often made matters worse as their effects wore off and I found myself back on the street.

These four foundations are the *roots* of a human being. What they need is nurturing. No substitute will do. If you are not at peace and ease, then the source of your dis-ease will be found in these foundations. All forms of disease (physical and non-physical) can be traced back to your Health, Home, Family and Work. They nurture your physical and spiritual condition.

Many of you have these foundations in place, others may view them as mundane or dismiss them as obvious. Think again. Ask yourself: am I living in peace and ease in Paradise? If you are not, then consider any one of your physical and spiritual needs. You will find that your needs will be met by nurturing one or more of the foundations. Health, Home, Family and Work are physical *and* spiritual in their nature. They are intimately connected in the process of nurturing the whole human being. Try this. The next time your soul is crying out, look and you will see that both the cause and the cure lies within these foundations.

In the same way, when we look at the condition of humanity, we can see why millions are suffering on the Earth. The way to promote world peace and ease is by helping ourselves and each other to develop our foundations of living.

The time has come to create *Pan Paradise* on Earth, but how do we help billions of people to create their ideal Health, Home, Family and Work? What humanity now needs to evolve is to embrace the simplest and easiest way to procreate healthy foundations of living. What is that? So far, humanity has mainly used physical activity to create and control our environment. This is why nine tenths of our minds lie dormant! Too much physical activity is now destroying the body of humanity and the Earth. We need to open our minds and discover new methods of changing our current conditions and creating new realities.

I am going to introduce you to what I call *The Panlife Process** of manifesting your dreams (metaphysical) into (physical) reality. The Panlife Manifestation Process uses The Pan Pathways and symbols to regulate the interaction between the physical and metaphysical. Our environment is composed of the interaction between the physical and non-physical. As we already know, we use the pathways of Being, Knowing, Relating and Creating to channel our energy from one entity to another. This energy can be concentrated to manifest what we wish via the use of symbols. A symbol is a very powerful object as it represents images which originate from deep within us. For example, a staff is a stick, but it also represents the truth in many traditions.

A symbol is therefore both physical and non-physical in nature, just like a human being. A symbol stands for or takes the place of something. We can manifest what a symbol represents by focusing our energies on it. Many people already use objects as symbols without knowing it, to manifest what they desire. Teenagers use posters and adults status symbols to attract what they desire. Religions and organisations use logos and buildings to attract what they want. In the same way, we can manifest whatever we need and want with the use of symbols.

I want to begin by showing you how to connect the pathways towards manifesting your basic needs via symbols. The Pan Pathways leading from your centre are the pathways of Being, Knowing, Relating and Creating. When you choose a symbol which represents what you desire, the power from your being activates the symbol via the pathways and manifests it in the material world. I suggest you try the process yourself.

---

* Panlife Process taken from the Panlife teachings by Raja.

Panlife Manifestation Process

1. Close your eyes and slowly take several deep breaths until you feel completely relaxed.

2. Now take a good look at the diagram on the opposite page and imagine what it would feel like to have perfect health, a beautiful home, a loving family and a fulfilling work life.

3. For each of the foundations of living: Health, Home, Family and Work, choose a symbolic object. For Home it could be a plaque reading *Home Sweet Home.* For Health, a mirror; family, a photo; and work, a lamp.

4. Choose a symbolic object for each of the four pathways of Being, Knowing, Relating, and Creating, e.g. a stone for Being, a crystal for Knowing, a telephone for Relating and a candle for Creating.

5. Close your eyes again and visualise yourself placing these symbolic objects in and around your home. You can start with Knowing at the front door, which signifies the gateway to Paradise. Then gather these symbolic objects within a definite time and place them where you live.

6. Each day contemplate on what you want each symbol to manifest in that aspect of your life. Make sure you concentrate your energy on what you *really need.* As you focus on each symbol, you will begin to attract that which you need, in ways you previously did not think possible.

7. If the symbols you have activated are not manifesting in your life, then you have to examine your motive and resistance to attracting that which you need. For example, a very educated or spiritual person may be able to talk with great wisdom, but be unable to manifest because of the fear and doubt within, whereas a simple person can often manifest miracles.

Pray and ask God to guide you.

The Panlife Personal Oracle

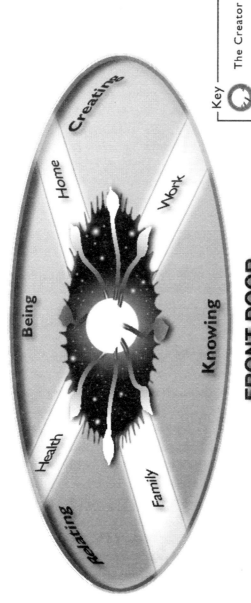

FRONT DOOR

The placement of symbols activates an oracle of energy and consciousness. As you focus on the symbols, the oracle will increase in intensity until it reaches critical mass. It will then draw from all spheres what you have identified with each symbol.

Symbols are a method of touching your inner reality. Like touchstones, they are highly charged objects which activate the law of attraction. Every object is a symbol – a source of energy which radiates and attracts. Be aware of the objects you bring into your life, as they determine the condition of your being.

A symbol is a point of unity between your inner and outer world. The placement of symbolic objects and images connects the subconscious with the outside world. A symbolic object is charged with thoughts and emotions. Symbolic objects and images become activated by strong thoughts and emotions which then manifest as physical objects, conditions or events in your life. When thoughts or emotions reach a certain intensity, they become magnetic and attract whatever you are focusing on into the given space. Symbols regenerate our minds and determine our behaviour. Much of the cultural schizophrenia we have is due to the lack of appropriate symbols in our lives.

Symbols are at the heart of our lives.

Be aware that the symbols and images you connect with will be *manifested* in your life. By contemplating specific images related to your Home, Health, Family and Work, you bring to the forefront of your mind what will become physical in form.

In ancient times, our species used stones and carvings to initiate this law of creation. Once the symbolic objects and images are placed, 'the force' remains activated until it is manifested or consciously changed. The energy must be activated with great intensity and contemplation, otherwise it will fade and become dormant. The intensity of your thoughts and emotions, on the symbolic objects and images, is vital in the process of physical materialisation. When you have materialised the symbol in the physical form, it will vanish from your desire. This process will continue again and again until there is a void. It may seem that without symbols we would be non-beings, but this is natural since the bodies in which we exist are themselves symbolic objects.

By playing with symbols, you are changing your inner and outer environment. The nature of symbols can serve, both as an indication of the state of your environment, and your state of consciousness within it. Therefore the same object, at different stages of your life, can appear differently and the meaning of a symbol will change as your consciousness becomes multidimensional.

Take a look around your home and you will see how much the physical (material) and the metaphysical (spiritual) are linked. Take a close look at your front door, at where you cook and eat, sleep and bathe and then see how the objects and images you have affect your Home, Health, Family and Work. Your life is a reflection of the objects and images that you love.

Our home is the reflection of the self.

When we see the Earth as our home and humanity as the occupant, what do we see? Go to any city and you will see the symbolic objects and images upon which its culture is focused. As you look closer, observe their effect on people. We live in a world where people worship *form* and neglect the *formless*. The present world culture is focusing on great achievements: building bigger, higher and faster. Behind most great achievements, however, there are often feelings of fear and insecurity. People who are happy and fulfilled do not need to prove themselves. They simply live and let live. They just know what they need and do not need.

How much of what we have in our homes, streets, schools and churches do we really need in order to be happy? Our culture is falling down like a house of cards, because we are neglecting the very foundations of our lives, for the sake of collecting more and more material objects and money.

The symbolic objects and images you have chosen will reveal to you your focus in life and how you have come to be in your present position. This is your big opportunity, for the gates of Paradise await you. *Be strong and fear not*. Let go of all that you do not need because it is stopping you from entering Paradise. Have faith, and focus *only* on tending to your foundations of living. Soon you will witness a personal paradise. Your personal paradise will then extend to your family, community, country and on ever expanding levels. Imagine what you can manifest with The Panlife Process. In the future the means of materialising our desires will merge symbology with technology.

My aim here is to introduce you to the power of Panlife and the means to activate its use. The purpose of this explanation is to reinstate the belief that you have the power to create anything imaginable, including paradise. The Panlife Process can be used to manifest what we want on the personal and planetary level. I am going to use these examples to demonstrate the power of The Panlife Oracle.

1) The Panlife Oracle has played a key role in my life and work on the planet. Over the years its awesome potential has increased in intensity. That is why The HELP Programme is prospering miraculously, without a movement, evangelism, marketing or hype. The HELP book was created via The Panlife Manifestation Process.

2) On the 11th of January '98 I was invited by a close friend to a birthday celebration. We were to meet on a small hill overlooking her estate. When I arrived, there were four friends around a fire and I could sense peace and ease. There was little said, but soon we became aware that we were stood close to one of the symbolic objects used to activate The Panlife Oracle in October '95. Since then, the whole energy of the property and people has changed radically for the better, to the point of periodic paradise.

Panlife
is the way
to
Paradise.

3) In 1985, I was led by God to go and activate The Panlife Oracle in West Berlin. The reason being: the Berlin Wall was in the way of God's work on Earth and the Brandenburgh Gate had to be opened before HELP could reach people behind *The Iron Curtain.* The people in the communist countries were suffering because their leaders had blocked God's help from reaching those who were praying for God's help. The first step was to pray near the Brandenburgh Gate and along the wall, which was built by the communists after the Second World War. As I prayed, I realised the need to bring down the wall and without *bloodshed.* On a cold winters day in 1986, I activated The Panlife Oracle in Berlin by placing the appropriate symbols, starting near the Brandenburgh Gate, which symbolised Knowing – the door to Paradise. From then on, I lived at Sonnenallee, Neuköelln, and visited Berlin every few weeks to teach at the Phad Centrum and pray while walking around The Panlife Oracle. On the 3rd of October 1989 the Berlin Wall came down without bloodshed.

As you practise The Panlife Process correctly, the power of God will flow through your Being, Knowing, Relating and Creating, manifesting Health, Home, Family and Work. The Foundations of HELP are also The Foundations of Pan Paradise on Earth. Rooted in God, you will choose appropriate symbols to nurture the roots of being human. The human being is the most powerful symbol on the Earth: that is why *you* can affect the direction of this planet.

The Panlife Process will play a key role in the creation of Pan Paradise on Earth.

In the past few years I have been preparing to activate a Global Panlife Oracle which I will expose in the future. A place called Pan Paradise has been created on this Earth. From this place, my condition of being is activating the Global Panlife Oracle. The two things I will leave behind are the *place* and the *consciousness* to create Pan Paradise on ever expanding levels.

Raja praying and giving thanks at the Brandenburgh Gate.

United in prayer at a HELP Seminar in Germany.

Photo: Robert Reile, Summer 1989

238

Resistance to Paradise

Now that I have told you about The Panlife Process as the method for creating Pan Paradise on Earth, do you have any resistance to living in paradise? I am going to ask you a question. Let your answer be a simple yes or no.

Do you live in peace and ease – Paradise?

Your resistance to paradise is reflected in the extent of peace and ease in your life. Resistance is driven by *fear* which leads to illusion and denies you peace and ease. In turn, a lack of peace and ease breeds fear and increases resistance to paradise.

The *first* step to overcoming your resistance is to *believe,* to transform fear into the faith that paradise is possible. *Every* idea, thought, emotion and action is motivated by either fear or faith. Even though I have told you the way to create paradise, it is your fears that will deny you paradise. To overcome the fear of paradise you have to believe and be helped to understand the nature of fear. In helping people create paradise, I have discovered that there are two basic kinds of fear.

- *Fear of the known*
- *Fear of the unknown*

Fear of the known comes from anticipating what will happen to you. If, for example, you were abused by your parents, then you may fear intimate relationships with other adults. Fear of the known may also be learnt through observation and can be as crippling as having undergone the actual experience yourself. Many of us are afraid of sharks, snakes, bats, black men, the dark, sexual disease, death, not because we have been harmed by them, but because of what others have told us. Make a list of your top ten fears and see if they have actually happened to you.

Most of your fears will never happen.

Fear and doubts are like ghosts in our minds. They can prevent us from moving forward. Even the smallest fear can cripple the most powerful spiritual people. Look closely at your fears and see how much the way you live and your future is controlled by them. Although both kinds of fear can paralyse its victims, I have found that the fear of the unknown is the worst.

Fear of the unknown is exactly opposite to fear of the known . Its victim is not aware of what the fear is, where it comes from and what its consequences might be. If, for example, a mother has a deep fear of the dark, she can pass this fear on to her children, even though she may neither mention it nor tell them to go into the dark. Unlike the fear of the known, which is passed on by what we say and do, the fear of the unknown is passed on by what we *don't say and don't do*. But why should you fear the unknown? What makes you assume that the unknown will harm you?

Having overcome my own resistance to paradise, I realised that it was not the fear of harm that was at the core, but the fear of becoming more creative and comfortable. Let me explain. Since I had become homeless at fourteen years of age, I had already faced and overcome fears of adverse conditions and hardship, homelessness, hunger, poor health, sleeplessness, violence and death. I had mastered every adversity that humanity had to offer and yet I felt unsafe and fearful. That fear was one of being without suffering, that is, of the unknown, in my case, the fear of total peace and ease, of Paradise.

I have come to realise that the fear of becoming comfortable (change for the better) originates from deep within the recesses of the human psyche and the collective human consciousness. The human species has become masterful at managing adversities and crisis, such as disease, famine, wars, slavery, rape, mass starvation, suicide, murder and pollution. How is it possible that a species with such imagination, creativity and competence has never managed to experience a unitary world living in peace and ease?

We take comfort in adversity. However brutal the knocks, it becomes the affirmation of what we think we are. Addicted to it, we return again and again to the source of our pain. Without it we are nothing. We deserve it. We have such a disease that its cure has to be truly horrific. We are prisoners of this fate and, like many real-life prisoners, we can no longer visualise life without confinement and powerlessness. At the first prospect of freedom, we re-offend, content to go back to the safety of our punishment, the truth of our inadequacy, the pleasure of our pain.

Is it possible that the fear of the unknown, in this scenario the unknown Paradise, is forcing us all to keep recreating more and more adverse conditions in order for us to feel 'safe'? How often do we destroy something just before it reaches the point of fulfilling us? The unspoken fear of total joy and comfort has been passed on from generation to generation and has become so rife that some people are now preparing to cope with Armageddon! The fear of paradise is so deep and powerful that if anyone even mentions the word Paradise, they are ridiculed, sabotaged and even murdered.

In all these years of teaching about Pan Paradise, I have found that people's resistance to paradise brings out the worst in them. The fear of the unknown paradise is so deeply rooted that it overrides one's reason, integrity and belief. I am certain that Jesus was crucified because he said, *"I have come to build the Kingdom of Heaven on Earth."* Even those who believe in paradise are crippled by their fears from actually creating paradise. The most resistance to paradise has come from the deeply spiritual, who believe in a Heavenly Paradise, but not as a reality here and now.

Many years ago, I was on a train and in the same compartment with a preacher. After a while he asked me, *"Do you believe in God?"* Our conversation soon lead to the suffering state of humanity. So, I introduced him to The Pan Pathways and the Way to Paradise. Whilst he agreed with the simple logic of The Pan

Pathways as the way to create paradise, he began to resist its implications for his own life and his religious belief. He did not believe that paradise was possible on Earth. The more I explained how simple and practical it was to create a living paradise, the more resistance he showed to my suggestion and me. The further I revealed the way to paradise, the more his resistance increased.

To get an understanding of what I am saying, try this. The next time you are with people you know, introduce them to the idea of Paradise. Observe. Go further and put forward the nature of paradise and the way to create it. Explain how simple and practical the creation of paradise can be. Watch their reaction as you go further on The Pathway of Paradise and then openly share that your life is paradise. Express wholeheartedly what it feels like to live in a condition of total peace and ease. You will get a range of reactions, from acceptance to ridicule, and envy to total rejection. Whenever you take people into the realm of paradise, they are entering into a world which is beyond *their worst nightmare*. The human psyche has rarely experienced paradise and the built up fears over the ages come to the fore, as people come face to face with a complete unknown – Paradise.

Be aware of the fears and strong resistance you will encounter, both from within yourself and from without. That resistance will manifest in the form of sabotage. By sabotage I mean whatever prevents you from living in peace and ease. Overcoming the sabotage from within and from other people will bring forth the wisdom which will enable you to help others create their paradise. Be careful however, with whom you share your views especially in the early stages. Sabotage is a subtle phenomenon.

For over two decades whilst I was teaching The Pan Pathways, I did not reveal the true purpose of these pathways. Then, the time came for me to openly proclaim that The Pan Pathways will accelerate Human Evolution and Life Procreation. In effect to create Paradise on Earth.

My soul purpose of being on the Earth
Is to help create peace and ease – Paradise.

At first, most people I know were stunned, then the message began to sink into their subconscious. The sabotage began with my friends. It is often the people you grew up with who resist the most, when your life starts to become paradise. If you tell them, the response is often, *"well, who do you think you are?"* When this happens, be quiet and stand with God. Saint Paul said, *"A wide door of opportunity appears before me and with it many adversaries."* When Joseph had a dream and told his brethren, they hated him the more!

Have you ever asked yourself how the saints and prophets were not able to create paradise even with their followers? Examine closely the life of any figure who proclaimed the coming of Paradise on Earth and you will open the door to a very strange phenomenon – *Sabotage*. Sabotage manifests in infinite forms and formless ways from within and without. All forms of sabotage originate from the *conscious* and *unconscious*.

Conscious sabotage originates from the conscious level of mind and manifests itself in many forms from apathy to assassination. This type of sabotage is of form and can be identified by the damage done. For example, the assassination of Martin Luther King was brilliantly planned and executed. His message evoked such fear in those who supported the "status quo" that they had to kill him. Assassination is one extreme of conscious sabotage. The other is simply apathy. Throughout the ages, messengers have come and gone, yet, even those who have worked with them fell asleep soon after their departure. Even the heads of church and state do not act upon the message of their prophets.

Unconscious sabotage originates from the unconscious level of the mind and manifests in formless ways, from negligence to betrayal. What would happen for example, if you declared to your family and friends that you are on The Pathway of Paradise and will devote your life to helping other people create Paradise on Earth? I have found that even those who believe in the creation of paradise begin to sabotage in ways of which they themselves are not even aware. The need to sabotage paradise originates from deep within the human psyche, in the unconscious mind. What an individual or institution believes on a conscious level is not necessarily what motivates their decisions and action. Have you ever asked yourself why so many are suffering when so many believe in God?

I have found that it is often those who are the 'wisest' and understand what I am saying and what I stand for, that resist my message. Coming face to face with a person living in a condition of paradise can be very frightening. The 'light' is too bright for most people to withstand. I can best explain this by the following analogy.

Imagine that you are swimming in the sea with dolphins on a bright warm day. On the surface the water is clear and the dolphins are friendly. There is so much love and joy that your whole being is vibrating like a golden ball of light. As you dive deeper, the water gets colder and darker. The surrounding is more hostile, since here life forms hurt each other. In the world of hunter-hunted, life is ruled by fear of lack and attack. In the same way the world we live in exists on different levels. Be aware of the effect you will have on people as you walk on the Pathways to Paradise.

As you walk on the Pathways to Paradise, the moments of peace and ease will increase from day to day. The duration of paradise in your life will increase as you *remember* and *recreate* the condition of peace and ease. There will come a time when you will live in Paradise continually. When that happens you will have become a **Panhuman** (whole light being) radiating peace and ease wherever you go. Your life will be paradise and you will help others to live in paradise.

Helping Each Other

Everyday I am amazed at how many times the word help is used in many situations. Go into any shop or reception and the first words you usually hear are *"How can I help you?"* Phone any charity or service organisation and the word help will be central to the call. Observe any commercial broadcast on the television and you will be surprised how often the word *help* is used. Why?... Helping each other is central to human existence.

Helping each other makes our lives easier, more comfortable and prosperous. Common sense tells us that the more we help each other, the more comfortable our lives will become in every situation imaginable. Is it possible that by helping each other constantly, we can make our lives easier, more peaceful and prosperous, to the point of Paradise? If this is true, then helping each other on the one-to-one and nation-to-nation levels is the solution to our crises and the way to create Pan Paradise on Earth.

Is helping each other the way to create Pan Paradise on Earth?

Could the creation of Pan Paradise on Earth be *based* on the simple activity of *'helping each other'*? Yes. Every action you perform either helps or harms yourself and others. To help is to heal and to harm is to hurt! Every time we help, we take a step closer to 'Heaven' and many steps will take *all of us* to a living Paradise on Earth. You may ask, *"Isn't help common sense?"* Yes, but not the process and potential of HELP as revealed here.

Evolution often happens in leaps. When something new is revealed we wonder why *we* didn't see what is now so clear. The bible says, *"God will create a new thing,"* and that is the discovery of HELP. One miraculous new thing HELP will do is to fulfil the mission of Jesus and take him off the cross. Jesus went to the cross to build the Kingdom of Heaven on Earth and by building the Heavenly Paradise, we shall help Jesus off the cross.

The goal of helping Jesus off the cross may seem impossible and even blasphemous, but I know that by helping each other we shall do exactly that. The bible says that *"Jesus despised the cross"*. For how long do you want to continue the suffering of Christ? The time has come to take Christ off the cross. Jesus came to help humanity and now we must help him off the cross. The bible says, *"Look after one another"*. But so many spiritual people do not have the time, money and energy to help others. Do you have the same problem of lack?

If you have a lack of time, money and energy it is because you are not helping others! Many people are scraping the barrel because they do the bare minimum to help each other. Well, it is especially when you do not have the time, money or energy that you should help others. When you need help in any aspect of your life, ask God to help you. Then expect help from others. If other people are not helping you, then help them. Why? By helping others you will release the indwelling Spirit of God. Being helpful will benefit others, but you will benefit more than anyone.

The next time you are lacking in anything be aware that you are neglecting to help. When this happens, find ways to help others with whatever you have and in any way you can. Have the courage to step out in faith, by helping others above and beyond the bare minimum. By helping others above and beyond what is expected, God will do *for you*, above and beyond what you can imagine. If that is true, then helping each other will turn poverty into prosperity and suffering into salvation. Helping each other is the way we shall overcome all our crises on the planetary and personal level.

Whether you are rich or poor you cannot live without help from others. Look at how much your life depends on others and

*HELP is the solution
to our crisis
and the way to create
Pan Paradise on Earth.*

how much they need your help. We are on constant *stand by* to help and be helped by others, or to harm and be harmed by others. Today you will have a choice to use your time, money and energy to help or harm. But how will you know the difference between help and harm? Well, help will heal and unite, whereas harm will hurt and disunite. Mother Teresa for example, went to India to help the poor and diseased. She went to help, not to convert, preach, change or dominate people. By devoting her life towards helping people, Mother Teresa healed thousands and united billions around the world. The simple helpful actions of this little, frail woman touched people from all races and religions, bringing unity within humanity. From a very early age I have been inspired by Mother Teresa and learnt that one person can help countless millions, without position or organisations. In the same way, we can help each other, regardless of our differences.

HELP will unite all races and nations to create one world with God.

Why, you may ask, do we need to bring God into the creation of one world? Well, without God, we are cut off from the *source* of help, and that is why billions are helpless today. The crisis within humanity is not due to the lack of money, technology, resources or know how, but due to the void – lack of God's help in people's lives. The bible says, *"The holy spirit is on stand by"*. Stand by for what? To help you! Without God's help, we have to rely on our own efforts and look where that is taking our species!

If you do not follow God's will, then whose will do you follow? All of us have to serve a master and history has shown time and again that any rule other than God's will be government by Tyranny. So, when I say one world under God, *I do not* mean one government, but one world governed by the will of God. But what is the will of God? *The will of God is that all your needs are met.*

When all your needs are met – that is Paradise. In the coming epoch, God will guide us directly on the individual and collective levels to govern, and together we shall unite under the spirit of God. The Way of HELP will play a central role in the salvation of humanity and the creation of Pan Paradise on Earth.

HELP is the way to save our souls.

HELP is neutral, practical and universal in its capacity to heal, save and unite people in the most difficult situations. For example, when you are in a crisis, you call emergency. The response from the operator is, "Can I help you?" In the same way, God helps those who cannot help themselves. The one universal *need* of all life forms is help. Without help life falls apart and with help we reinstate life. Hence, by helping one life form, we help all life forms everywhere.

As we enter the next millennium, our species is in crisis. The only way we shall overcome all our problems is by helping each other. Helping each other will be the touchstone that will enable humans to evolve from hunter-hunted to helper-helped, and into what I call **Panhumans***. Helping each other will carry our species from its current crisis to the next order of existence, thus beginning a new cycle of Human Evolution and Life Procreation. Looking into the future, we can see how HELP will enable our species to create a world where people help each other and live in harmony.

---

* Panhuman: taken from the Panlife teachings, meaning *whole light being.*

249

The

HELP

Programme

The Role of HELP

To cut a long story short, our species has made a mess of itself and the Earth. The irony is that, despite all our spiritual and scientific knowledge, we have a crisis on our hands. Why? What is the cause of the crisis? When we ask the experts, they all give us a different explanation. Has our species made a mess as part of a learning process, or have we deliberately set out to destroy ourselves and the Earth? Is our species about to end its life span or are we about to enter a new evolutionary spiral which will take us into a *new way* of evolution?

If you look at the human species from an evolutionary perspective, then our species as it stands today is in its infancy. For instance, when we compare ourselves with the origin of life on Earth, some three billion years ago, then our species with less than ten million years on the Earth, is the equivalent of a child learning to walk. Is it surprising that human beings are stumbling and making a mess of things? What humanity needs now, is evolutionary guidance at this critical age. The time has come for us to *grow up*, clean up the mess and move on to enter the next stage of our evolutionary journey. On this basis of understanding, *all* our problems can be seen, and solved, as part of one crisis, the crisis in human evolution.

The crisis is evolution.

The solution is evolution.

The challenge is to help our species evolve.

At every stage of our evolutionary journey, there has been what we call a crisis. In fact the nature of evolution is crisis concurrent with transformation – change. The species that does not adapt to the crisis dies. The difference between the current crisis and those in our past, is the real threat to our existence, and that of the Earth. We have reached a point where our species has to change from the old way of hunter-hunted to helper-helped.

The Role of HELP is to *change* the evolutionary direction of humanity in this way. The HELP Process is the *solution for evolution* that will enable us to move from competition to co-operation. To change the course of human evolution from hunter to helper is not a 'quick fix', even though we have the method to make it happen. We shall need the co-operation of *key* individuals and organisations to spread The HELP Process worldwide.

HELP all around the world.

The Role of The HELP Programme is to communicate The HELP Process to individuals and organisations all around the world. The mission of HELP has a long way to go before The HELP Process is taught and practised in the mainstream. It may take another forty years or more to diffuse HELP. This is a long time considering the crisis we face now. HELP may look slow, but it is the fastest way for us to change our condition. The HELP Programme is like a tree which will grow slowly at first, but it will surely bear fruit and fulfil its God-given mission.

As we approach the year 2000, many people are praying and believing, expecting something to happen that will help humanity. The introduction of HELP will help humanity in *every* aspect of our existence. To understand what I am saying, consider *any* evolutionary obstacle and you will find that HELP is central in finding the solution. HELP promotes Human Evolution and Life Procreation. By using HELP consciously, we begin to *procreate our evolution* with a God-given purpose – Pan Paradise.

Procreative Evolution

So far, our species have been relying on 'trial and error' to survive the rigours of our evolutionary journey. That is why millions of people have been killed and hundreds of other species have disappeared. Now we cannot justify such behaviour, as we have become conscious of evolution from a universal perspective. Mere survival because of chance or accidentally avoiding war is no longer acceptable. So perhaps now, we shall be able to decide what is universally desirable for humanity in the future, and work to evolve consciously, rather than by accident.

Some like to think that, all the way through history, there has been a vital force at work, striving for perfection and this will still modify the changes to come. Others conceive life as struggling upward to form ever more integrated wholes: for example, a cell is a more perfect whole than a crystal. Whatever one believes, our species needs to take a major leap in order to save itself and the Earth from destruction.

Looking back at the origin of our species, it seems that we have taken major leaps in our evolution, i.e., from Homo Habilis to Homo Erectus. The leap we are about to take however, is going to separate us from the animal kingdom once and for all. In essence we are going to become a new species whose consciousness is not grounded in survival, i.e., hunter-hunted, which has been the driving force behind our evolution. We have reached a critical point in our evolutionary journey, where we must take a quantum leap from hunter to helper and competition to co-operation.

The new way of co-existing has been developing for thousands of years in isolated pockets around the world. The fact that people understand and use the content of this book shows our readiness for the leap. What we need now is an actual process that will enable each one of us to participate in a worldwide programme of co-operation. The HELP Programme is based on what I have termed Procreative Evolution, where those living procreatively co-operate consciously towards creating our future. The process of *Procreative Evolution* is based on four basic principles:

~ **World Vision of the Future**

~ **Communication of the Vision**

~ **Leadership that Empowers by Example**

~ **Co-operation in a Worldwide Programme**

The HELP Programme is unique, as it enables *you* to use these principles and participate in procreative evolution without having to join an organisation or make a financial or material contribution. The HELP Programme calls upon individuals to help each other, not on their membership. The truth is you are already a member of humanity and to join or pay for procreative evolution is a contradiction in terms. Each one of us is not a member or part of evolution, *we are* human evolution! The HELP Programme is not an organisation, cult or religion, it is an educational method which presents the most common tools and methods for promoting procreative evolution. Your contribution to procreative evolution begins with discovering a world vision for our future.

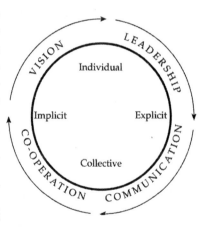

Vision of the Future

The first thing we need is a world vision. Although human societies differ greatly in culture, religion, history, politics and tradition, we need to have one vision that *unites* humanity. Why? A vision gives us direction! The bible says, *"where there is no vision, the people perish"*. What we need is a world vision that is so simple and universal that people from *all paths* can embrace it. A vision that does not call on people to conform, but to co-operate wholeheartedly because it serves their needs.

Pan Paradise as the world vision.

Why Pan Paradise? Because God wants to meet the need of every person. When humanity's needs are met, that is Pan Paradise. Imagine a world culture where each individual knows the world vision and can participate in its creation. The way to create Pan Paradise is to help each individual to focus on Health, Home, Family and Work. When we meet our *own needs* without compromising, we sow the seeds for future generations and meet their needs.

There are those who will say, *"but what about the destruction of the natural habitat, global warming, over-population, nuclear war?"* When human beings satisfy their *natural needs*, we shall cease all actions which are harmful and destructive to our natural habitat. The world vision of Pan Paradise depends on the well-being of *your* Health, Home, Family and Work, which brings peace and ease. When this happens we shall live in harmony and witness the creation of Pan Paradise.

The world vision of Pan Paradise does not overwhelm or alienate the individual because the way it works is easy to relate with. If you agree *wholeheartedly* with the world vision of Pan Paradise, then share the vision with those who will help to form a support group. Every group is composed of individuals and the entire human population is made up of individual groups. Individuals and groups will play a central role in the communication and creation of Pan Paradise.

Communication of the Vision

The secret of Procreative evolution is a procreative population. The question is: how can The HELP Programme communicate the world vision of Pan Paradise worldwide without an organisation? We could use magazines, books, tapes, and television, just as other organisations, but even the largest organisations cannot communicate their products worldwide, let alone create Pan Paradise.

Can HELP communicate the world vision
of Pan Paradise without an organisation?

Yes. By helping each other to build The Foundations of HELP, we change and transform our condition of crisis into one of peace and ease, Paradise. The secret is in the universal nature of the activity of *helping* and the primal need to build The Foundations of *HELP*. Here are two examples of how The HELP Process will work to *build* the world vision of Pan Paradise.

First: Bees build their hives without any organised control from the queen bee and yet *all* the bees work together towards a common goal. This is called *divergent* behaviour. Humans can also use divergent behaviour to create a world vision where everyone is working together without being controlled by an individual or organisation. Helping each other is the key activity that is universal in divergent behaviour.

Second: The HELP Programme does not have *a* leader or following, an organisation or hierarchy, buildings or databases, and yet HELP continues to spread. How? Just as the bees are playing their part in building a bee hive, humans are helping each other to build their Health, Home, Family and Work, The Foundations of Pan Paradise.

HELP is communicated from person to person via helpful actions. The more you help others the more others will help you. In this way you are taking part in a world-wide programme for creating Paradise here and now. That is how HELP is communicating a world vision of Pan Paradise.

Leadership that Empowers by Example

As our world becomes more complex, turbulent and unpredictable, there is a need for highly committed and competent people. This applies at all levels of society, particularly where people need the most help. In these times of crisis people look to their leaders for inspiration and guidance, but they look in vain. Are your leaders egotistical, using their self appointed position to control and exploit people for selfish motives? When I said this at a seminar, a man stood up and asked me, *"What is your idea of leadership?"*

A guide dog helping a blind woman across the street.

True leaders, such as Buddha, Jesus, Mohammed, Gandhi and Mother Teresa, led by taking the lowest position. True leadership consists of actions which have transcended greed and glamour and become functions of honesty, humility and service. All true leaders have these qualities in common which they use through love, truth, kindness and compassion to help other people. It is their ability to help fellow humans that gives them the right to be leaders. The moment we utter the words, *"How can I help you?"* we take the position of service and thus become a leader. *We are all leaders.*

What humanity needs now are leaders who are *anointed* and who operate in the will of God. Many people are anointed to lead, but do not have the *faith* to follow the will of God. A true leader is one who demonstrates absolute faith by manifesting the power of God. Imagine how much *one* true leader could do for humanity with the power of God! The bible says, *"One with God is more than the majority."* One person can change the situation of their community, country and the world. Today, there are approximately 120 countries that have a national leader. Are these leaders appointed or anointed? The world vision of Pan Paradise depends on people who are aware of their anointing and help to lead our species according to the will of God.

Co-operation in a Worldwide Programme

Human beings are social beings. We need the help of others to survive the rigours of society. We find that tasks are easier, projects get completed in less time and the fruits of labour are multiplied when individuals co-operate. Many facets of modern life, however, often separate people from each other. Personal transportation, telephones and televisions, separate people from face-to-face contact. These technological advances are trade-offs which have seeded an alienation, a loneliness, a longing for belonging and a striving for identity. The media preys on this incessantly, subtly implanting capitalist ideas and images in virtually every movie, advertisement and political broadcast.

The HELP Programme too, will use all means of communication including the media, yet the emphasis is on co-operation not coercion. With personal involvement, we are creating effective channels that best suit your needs and the needs of the community in which you live. Indeed, the word communication originates from community and communion, meaning, 'coming together and becoming one'. From communication comes co-operation which is a fancy word for helping each other.

Helping each other is the driving force behind procreative evolution. It results in natural networks that serve individual needs without exploitation or the use of coercion. In this sense, the notion of help (love) holds magical powers for creating a world living in peace and ease. From the moment we help each other, life becomes easier, and the more we help, the easier life becomes. Even something as simple as holding someone's hand can turn pain into living paradise. Each act of help is like a drop which slowly and gradually sends ripples around the world.

Procreative evolution links human consciousness to evolution. It provides the process that enables us to participate and take responsibility for our own future. Unlike animals, human beings have the capacity to comprehend a bigger picture in which they can consciously participate. Our ability to promote procreative evolution will speed up our evolutionary process and raise us to the next phase in our evolutionary journey.

During the coming epoch, humans will evolve into a new kind of creature. The ***Panhuman*** * will come into being. Their perception of life will not be based on fear and illusion but on faith and reality. As we move from illusion to reality, the duality that separates us will become unity. Panhumans will perceive the world as one. Matter and spirit, male and female, good and evil will be embraced by the ***Panlife*** * consciousness that all-is-one. This is the nature of the universe called ***Pantheism*** – Identification of God with the universe. Each one of us is knowingly or unknowingly involved in the greatest transformation since our species began to emerge from the animal realm.

We are the first creatures to become aware of our capacity to envision our future and create it. We are at the dawn of the creation of a new kind of creature, The Panhuman, who will roam the Earth freely and create one world which I call ***Pan Gaia***. The future looks bright and beautiful as we see the world with love. The new world is at hand and in our hands.

We need your participation.

*Panhuman: a whole light being.
*Panlife: from the Panlife teachings.

Participation

Many people write to us wanting to participate in The HELP Programme. People are used to participating by joining spiritual, political and environmental organisations. That is not The Way of HELP. Our work does not depend on an organisation with millions of members and followers.

> *The HELP Programme is not an organisation*
> *that you join. There is no membership or fee.*

So how do we participate? We participate by helping ourselves, each other, life forms and the Earth in our own way. This way of helping frees us from guilt and obligation, so we can exercise our free will. Each one of us can exercise our free will to help in both minor and major ways, *every* day. This can be from opening a door for someone to feeding millions. These are all ways of participating in The HELP Programme.

An act of help is an act of giving or serving without seeking glory or gain. By helping without the need of reward we activate the law of love and prosperity. Every act of help is the harbinger of peace, ease and prosperity. That makes helping a very rewarding activity and a way to prosper. The rewards of helping are found now and in the future. Firstly, there is the joy in knowing that we have helped. This is the reward in the present. Secondly, since the people we are helping now may not be able to reward us, the help we render will be rewarded indirectly in the form of blessings and will come back to us in the future. In the bible God says:

> *"If you help build my house, I will build yours."*

One act of help comes back many fold. If this is true, then the more we help, the more we are helped in return. Imagine what we human beings can create when each act of HELP is multiplied a hundred fold and returns to manifest? The true practitioner understands the power of HELP and manifests accordingly.

Participation in The HELP Programme is as follows:

~ **The Call to HELP**

~ **The Opportunity to HELP**

~ **The Understanding of HELP**

~ **The Responsibility to HELP**

The Call to HELP is the idea or impulse which inspires us to help. This call can come from within or without and we have to choose to ignore it or respond. We are all called to help, but the majority of people do not hear their calling because they have been out of touch for so long. Those that do, ignore the call for want of something else. *Help and humility go together*.

If you are ignoring your calling, you are forsaking the opportunity to love and prosper now and in the future. If you cannot hear your calling and want to, all you have to say is, *"God what is my calling?"* Then be quiet and listen. Once you hear your call, devote yourself to the calling. Hearing the call sets The HELP Process and power in motion. Help is a call one acts upon now, where life is happening. In this way, help reconnects us with other people in our own family and community, where there are opportunities for helping each other.

The Opportunity to HELP exists in every moment, and by seizing opportunities we take charge of our destiny. Many people are poor, not because they live in a poor country, but because they cannot see the opportunity to HELP each other and prosper. The willingness to HELP attracts countless opportunities, each laden with all that you need and want. For example, taking the opportunity to HELP clean up the local park also presents the chance to meet people who can help you in some way.

All too often we see or meet people who we feel connected to, but this chance encounter in the shopping mall, cafe, bus stop or post office etc., is lost. Such encounters are not born out of chance, but created by psychic forces. To make full use of these meetings, we have created the HELP Connect Card, which creates the link in those critical moments.

HELP CONNECT CARD®

HELP™

Name:_____

_____

_____

Tel:_____

**The HELP Connect Card is the missing link
in the process of bringing people together.**

Over the years, the numbers of people using the HELP Connect Card has increased and a HELP Network has evolved, which is connecting people in their local communities. By connecting with each other in this way, people *join hands* and look for opportunities to help and create a support network in their own society. HELP creates the tapestry of society, but HELP does not stop here. The ideas expressed in this book, need to weave and flow naturally at the local level.

The Understanding of HELP comes from helping and learning about The HELP Process. The Pathways of Being, Knowing, Relating and Creating enable us to understand and use The HELP Process consciously. HELP is neither a complex spiritual system nor a scientific principle which needs a lot of explanation. HELP is a simple act which can be understood and used by everyone. Most of what you need to understand about HELP can be learned from this book, the HELP Tapes and in conversation with your family and friends. Because HELP works for everyone and in every interaction, you and your people will be able to easily understand and relate to the potential of HELP.

My message is for the common people.
My aim is to promote the common good.

The reason HELP works with everyone and in every situation is because it is both practical and spiritual in nature. HELP nurtures all our physical and spiritual needs equally. This is why people from all races and religions can understand, use and unite by helping each other. HELP is so simple that everyone can understand it. It is so useful that no one can live without it. HELP is the key to bringing peace, ease and prosperity into our lives and society. When HELP is put to work, it becomes our responsibility to help our family, friends and society. Many people like the idea of creating a better society, but cannot or will not take the responsibility to help.

People either like or dislike responsibility because it is associated with reward, fame, sacrifice, burdens and martyrdom. Others run from responsibility because it means accountability or work. Why else is our community and country in such a poor condition? It is easy to blame other people for the state of our planet, but what are we doing to help change it? The bible says, *"many are called, but few are chosen"*. A lot of people are called to help, but few take the responsibility. Even the most capable and wealthy people are often wrapped up in themselves.

The Responsibility to HELP becomes clear in our minds when we can hear the call of help. Just as we hear the call of hunger, we can hear the call of help from society. The word responsibility stands for *response-ability*, the ability to choose one's response. Hence, the way we have chosen to respond, demonstrates our capacity to take responsibility in society. What kind of responsibility then, have we assumed and what good is it doing in the world? A politician for example, may take responsibility for a whole region, but what are the motives and the outcome?

Our aim is to educate the individual to become aware of their call to help and take responsibility to help promote the common good. Each one of us has come into the world to fulfil our responsibility and that begins with taking care of ourselves, our family and community. A human being has an enormous capacity for taking responsibility that can expand from the individual to communal, regional to trans-regional, national to global and on to universal. *All* of us are capable of taking responsibility on any level we choose, but our choice is often limited by ourselves and those around us.

The responsibility of HELP is to assist our species in moving from hunter-hunted to helper-helped. This process may take up to a thousand generations before The Way of HELP takes root in the human condition. Such a responsibility cannot be completed by one individual and will require the co-operation of millions who have to rise to the challenge.

People often tell us that they have never heard of The HELP Programme. Well now you have and you know what needs to be done! HELP is an *unseen wave* created by countless helpful ideas, thoughts, feelings and actions. The wave of The HELP Programme has now reached you, and with your participation, HELP can reach many more.

For over twenty-eight years I have been discovering and developing HELP and getting ready to take the responsibility of helping humanity to create Pan Paradise. I am aware that such a responsibility seems impossible to fulfil, but with God's help and by helping each other we can manifest the miraculous. What we need now are the *individuals* with the courage, faith and the will to take responsibility and co-operate in the creation of the world vision of Pan Paradise... ***Can I help?***

Further HELP

If you have been deeply moved by the message in this book, you will be propelled to act. To help you get started we offer the following:

~ *HELP Seminars*

The HELP Seminars were recorded live in London at the Wandsworth Business Village. They are available in a comprehensive audio cassette pack. These seminars are for those who want to accelerate their practice of The HELP Process. The HELP Seminars promote co-operation at home, schools, colleges, social services and in business. The HELP Seminar cassette pack is available at all good bookshops.

~ *HELP Support Groups*

These informal meetings are a great way to help each other or simply to be together. The HELP Support Groups promote a sense of belonging and provide mutual support in your community. If you want to start a HELP Support Group, we can send you a support group starter pack containing a comprehensive HELP Seminars Audio Pack, HELP books and HELP Connect Cards. Also included are instructions on how to start and manage a support group.

~ *HELP Coordinators*

Having read this book, you may feel inspired to devote your life towards helping people. For that purpose we conduct The HELP Training for coordinators. To work directly with The HELP Programme, write and include details and ways in which you can help with your time and resources.

HELP ~ P.O. Box 929 ~ Wimbledon ~ London ~ SW19 2AX ~ UK

E-Mail: helpbooksint@easynet.co.uk
www.helpbooksInt.com

Glossary

Anointing	a God-given purpose and authority
Being	to be-live with The Infinite Being
Be-live	live according to The Infinite Being
Discovery	via reasoning, imagining or direct knowing
Ease	a comfortable state of being
Ego	born of the realm of illusion
Faith	belief in one's own being… The Infinite Being
God	the omnipresent being
Harbinger	a pioneer or forerunner
Infinite Being	present everywhere and in every thing
Intuition	direct knowing from The Infinite Being
Miracle	a supernatural event or outcome
Metaphysical	beyond the physical
Pan	one complete whole
Pan Gaia	one world – Pan Paradise on Earth
Panhuman	a whole light being
Panlife	one life
Paradise	condition of peace and ease
Pathway	a way to get from here to there
Peace	a harmless state of being
Prayer	being in communion with The Infinite Being
Real time	as experienced in the condition of being
Supernatural	beyond natural, normal